PHANTOM GOURMET

Guide to
BOSTON'S BEST
RESTAURANTS
2008

St. Martin's Griffin

D0291589

To the Phantom Phans who have made our book a bestseller,

our television show a hit, and the Phantom Gourmet Food Festival

the most delicious party in history. If I could go public, I'd share a beer

and some chicken wings with each and every one of you.

———————————————

PHANTOM GOURMET GUIDE TO BOSTON'S BEST RESTAURANTS 2008. Copyright
© 2007 by Phantom Gourmet, Inc. All rights reserved. Printed in the United States of
America. No part of this book may be used or reproduced in any manner whatsoever
without written permission except in the case of brief quotations embodied in critical
articles or reviews. For information, address St. Martin's Press, 175 Fifth Avenue,
New York, N.Y. 10010.

www.stmartins.com

Library of Congress Cataloging-in-Publication Data

Phantom Gourmet.
    Phantom gourmet guide to Boston's best restaurants 2008 / The Phantom
Gourmet.
        p.   cm.
    ISBN-13: 978-0-312-37460-0
    ISBN-10: 0-312-37460-7
    1. Restaurants—Massachusetts—Boston Region—Guidebooks. 2. Boston
Region (Mass.)—Guidebooks. I. Title.
    TX907.3.M42P44 2007
    641.9409744'61—dc22   2007019289

First Edition: September 2007

10 9 8 7 6 5 4 3 2 1

Contents

"Great Ates" by Category

"Great Ates" by Location

PHANTOM GOURMET'S HANDY PRICE INDEX*

$	Cheap	Under $15
$$	Moderate	$15 to $24
$$$	Expensive	$25 and up

*based on an average entrée price

Acknowledgments

I've never met most of these people, but each one helped make this book possible. Without them, I might have to get a real job. Thanks!

Dan Andelman

Dave Andelman

Eddie Andelman

Mike Andelman

Phil Balboni

Evan Berenson

Ernie Boch, Jr.

Marti Breden

Tina "Bunny" Bucchiere

Monica Collins

Mindy d'Arbeloff

Dale Dorman

Kim Driscoll

Rich Fahey

Gayle Fee

Sean Finley

Bob Howard

Lou Imbriano

Claire Jones

Will Kussell

Kenny Lawrence

Patrick Lyons

Kelly Malone

Pete Masucci

Max and Zach

Wendy McMahon

Mayor Tom Menino

Tom Mercer

John Mitchell

David Moldawer

Hank Morse

Joe O'Donnell

Chris Palermo

Ed Piette

The PhanClub

Laura Raposa

Bill Ritchotte

Eric Sherman

Ed Sparks

Paul Sullivan

Steve Sweeny

George Tobia

Steve Uliss

Nick Varano

Mark Viveiros

Scott Whalen

Jasper White

The Wong Family

Zito and Jen

Introduction

You are holding the most user-friendly, informative, and accurate guide to the best restaurants in and around Boston. For less than the price of a fancy cocktail, this book will help you get the most out of your dining dollar every single day.

This second edition has the same useful format, divided into 60 Great Ate categories by craving (hot dog, steak, sandwich) and neighborhood (Back Bay, North Shore, Cambridge). For each category, I provide my eight favorite places. I'm featuring dozens of new restaurants, and I've added new topics like Guilty Pleasures, Top Tables, and Huge Portions. Don't forget: the index allows searching by restaurant name and location.

The Phantom Gourmet is all about food and fun. So while you can keep this guide in your desk or glove compartment, you may also want to read it in your recliner. For a good laugh and insider information on how to be a smart diner, check out the 88 Tasty Tips at the back of the book.

My advice is to buy this guide, have a Phantastic meal, and tell 'em the Phantom Gourmet sent you.

—*The Phantom Gourmet*
  Mysterious Restaurant Critic

"GREAT ATES"
by Category

Phantom's All-Time Favorites

GREAT ATE

THE GREATEST: **Wood-Fired Cooking**

Fore Street $$$
288 Fore St., Portland, ME, (207) 775-2717
www.forestreet.biz

Fore Street is one of the most rustic and romantic eateries in New England. Wood-fired cooking is their specialty, and it's all done in open view of the customer, sprawled across a soaring dining room of brick and dark wood. Pizzas come out of the brick oven topped with gourmet ingredients like roasted peppers, onions, and spinach. The roasted mussels bathe in so much almond garlic butter, you'll want an entire loaf of bread to sop up every drop. Tender dry-rubbed pork loins do laps on the turnspit, and the grill sizzles full of steaks, chops, and fish. For dessert, don't miss the warm apple tarte tatin with smoked bacon ice cream!

THE GREATEST: **Beach Eats**

Back Eddy $$$
1 Bridge Road, Westport, MA, (508) 636-6500
www.thebackeddy.com

Whether you arrive by boat or by car, the Back Eddy is the ideal summer restaurant. It's a classy clam shack that takes full advantage of local farms and fishermen in modern dishes like sausage stuffed clams with Tabasco aioli. Giant seared scallops are wrapped in applewood-smoked bacon, and the yellowfin tuna steak takes on an Asian theme with wasabi, soy sauce, and kimchi. The light, airy atmosphere includes a patio bar, so you can sip a gin and tonic just feet from the water.

THE GREATEST: **Be Seen Brunch**

Sonsie $$$
327 Newbury St., Boston, MA, (617) 351-2500
www.sonsieboston.com

Sonsie seems to have a dress code, and it's designer threads. The beautiful clientele pack the marble café tables, which offer a full view of Newbury Street through the French doors. Phantom goes for the eclectic brunch cuisine like thick French toast with rum bananas and caramel. The huevos rancheros are invigorating served with grilled chorizo sausage. And the brick-oven pizzas will warm you up for a dessert finale of individual chocolate s'mores. Sonsie offers one of Boston's liveliest social scenes, whether at the massive mahogany bar, in the European lounge with deep leather chairs, or around the big tables in the back.

THE GREATEST: Splurge

Sorellina $$$
1 Huntington Ave., Boston, MA, (617) 412-4600
www.sorellinaboston.com
Sorellina is hardly affordable, but this is the reservation to get when you're going all out . . . or someone else is picking up the bill. Extravagant Italian fare includes arancini rice balls filled with Jonah crabmeat. Homemade pasta is paired with Kobe beef meatballs, and sides like Parmesan truffle fries are so lip-smackingly delicious, you won't dare share. For dessert, the molten chocolate cake is served in an individual cast-iron pot with cinnamon ice cream. The striking modern décor includes backlit floor-to-ceiling murals and an all-white bar.

THE GREATEST: Maple Syrup

Parker's Maple Barn $
1316 Brookline Rd., Mason, NH, (800) 832-2308
www.parkersmaplebarn.com
At Parker's Maple Barn, tucked back in the woods, you can actually observe the maple syrup being made before sampling it yourself in the nineteenth-century barn and silo, which now serves as a charming restaurant. The country-style menu includes seven kinds of pancakes, including maple walnut, blueberry, and pumpkin. Their sweet signature is maple-glazed baby back ribs and fried eggs. Savored with some maple-roasted coffee and cinnamon rolls smothered in icing, it's worth the morning drive. Customers can buy tins of their maple syrup from the gift shop next door.

THE GREATEST: Fine! Fine! Dining

Arrows $$$
Berwick Rd., Ogunquit, ME, (207) 361-1100
www.arrowsrestaurant.com
When there's a $50-per-person cancellation fee, either you're being taken for a ride or you're in for something special. Arrows is the current record holder for Phantom's all-time highest restaurant rating, making it well worth the trip to Maine. Set amidst woods and gorgeous gardens, the eighteenth-century farmhouse is highly

romantic. Dressed-up diners duck into the wood-and-glass encased porch, where a sprawling birch tree and square lanterns illuminate the scene. The playful menu changes daily; 90 percent of the restaurant's produce is grown on the grounds and they cure their own ham and fish. Each entrée is actually four mini creations. Seasonal inspirations might include red wine and honey poached beef or cedar-plank salmon with rosemary rhubarb candy.

THE GREATEST: Italian Subs

Bob's $
324 Main St., Medford, MA, (781) 395-0400
www.bobsfood.com

Bob's is where you go when you're not on a diet. The Italian eats at this sandwich shop and specialty store are served big, fast, and cheap. They even sell a six-foot sandwich packing eight pounds of meat and cheese on a homemade loaf of braided bread. As for single-serving subs, they offer steak and cheese, tomato basil with mozzarella and prosciutto, and one of the best chicken Parms Phantom has ever tasted. Takeout platters include stuffed shells and meatballs, sausage cacciatore, and chicken piccata. The shelves are stocked with imported Italian goods, and Bob's makes fresh pasta with a $12,000 machine imported from Italy.

THE GREATEST: Dinner, Hayride, and Music

Golden Lamb Buttery $$$
499 Wolf Den Rd., Hillandale Farm, Brooklyn, CT, (860) 774-4423

Golden Lamb Buttery is an extraordinary country escape that features great home cooking. The husband-and-wife team are the best hosts that Phantom has ever found. They put guests in high spirits throughout cocktail hour in a charming barn filled with knick-knacks. Then, owner Bob Booth fires up his tractor as everyone piles in the back for a sing-a-long hayride. The live music continues in the dining room with an intimate dinner prepared by his rosy wife, Jimmie. The prix fixe menu is money well spent for an entire evening of farm entertainment and a three-course meal. Reservations required, cash only, jacket and tie for gentlemen.

Bakeries
GREAT ATE

THE GREATEST: Wedding Cakes

Montilio's $
638 Adams St., Quincy, MA, (617) 472-5500
www.montilios.com

Specializing in unforgettable wedding cakes, Montilio's has baked for icons like JFK, Queen Elizabeth, and Pope John Paul II. They do it all, from classy creations covered in frosting flowers to Elmo cupcakes. They'll top a chocolate cake with chocolate-dipped strawberries or whip up a whimsical gift-cake "wrapped" in frosting ribbons. All their shops are stocked with ready-to-eat sweets like M&M cookies and breakfast pastries, as well as cakes by the slice. Additional locations are in Brockton and Waltham.

THE GREATEST: Cupcakes

Lulu's Bake Shoppe $
227 Hanover St., Boston, MA, (617) 720-2200
www.lulusbakeshoppe.com

Lulu's Bake Shoppe may be in Boston's famous Italian District, but this isn't the place for cannoli and ricotta pie. This sweet little spot is packed with made-from-scratch cupcakes instead. Chocolate and vanilla are ever so moist, smeared with rainbow-colored buttercream icing. Red velvet is Phantom's favorite, followed by carrot cake cupcakes with cream cheese frosting. Lulu's also has a coffee bar and other all-American treats like cream puffs, chocolate chip cookies, sticky buns, whoopie pies, and specialty muffins in flavors like Boston cream.

THE GREATEST: Fresh Baked Bread

Iggy's Bread of the World $
130 Fawcett St., Cambridge, MA, (617) 924-0949
www.iggysbread.com

Iggy's is the loaf of choice at many Boston restaurants, and is sold at Shaw's and Whole Foods. Even with all that volume, they bake some of the best loaves around. Their hearth-baked bread is made twice a day using all-natural ingredients. Iggy's is known for affordable staples like country sourdough and seedless rye. It's worth a trip to their Alewife headquarters for pizza by the slice and baguette sandwiches filled with basil, tomato, and mozzarella. Sweet stuff includes chocolate croissants, chocolate oatmeal cookies, and the most amazing pecan sticky buns.

THE GREATEST: Birthday Cakes

Party Favors $
1356 Beacon St., Brookline, MA, (617) 566-3330
www.partyfavorsbrookline.com
This store is a party planner's paradise. Every inch of Party Favors is crammed with colorful piñatas, inflated balloons, and wrapping paper, and the air is suffused by the tantalizing aroma of fresh-baked goods. The on-site cake decorators are artists in the medium of pure buttercream frosting. Decorations are done by hand, including flowers, penguins, pigs, and turtles. They can whip up an amazing Oscar the Grouch cake or a chocolate espresso torte with mocha beans. Everything from wedding cakes to cupcakes gets the same attention.

THE GREATEST: Fruit Tart

Pastiche Fine Desserts $
92 Spruce St., Providence, RI, (401) 861-5190
www.pastichefinedesserts.com
Pastiche is a tantalizing dessert spot, turning out Phantom's favorite fruit tarts. A butter pastry shell is filled with vanilla custard and then topped off with fresh fruit like kiwi, blueberries, strawberries, and orange. The space is warm and inviting like a European café, with intimate tables and a working fireplace. Pastiche is stocked with superb sweets like orange chocolate Bavarian cake, Russian teacakes, biscotti, rugelach, and chocolate walnut truffle cookies. For sipping, you'll find coffee drinks, tea, chai, and rich hot chocolate.

THE GREATEST: Chocolate Buffet

Café Fleuri $$$
The Langham Hotel, 250 Franklin St., Boston, MA, (617) 451-1900
http://boston.langhamhotels.com
Technically it's not a bakery. But then, the Saturday Chocolate Bar at Café Fleuri is in a category all its own. From September through June, chocoholics reserve for the extravagant all-you-can-eat dessert buffet. The jaw-dropping spread includes cookies, cakes, tortes, fondue, and made-to-order crepes. There's quite a range, from dark chocolate mousse and truffle pops to the chocolate fountain and experimental chocolate sushi. Phantom can't resist the chocolate croissant pudding or the juicy strawberries dipped in white chocolate.

THE GREATEST: **Bite-Sized Pastry**

Konditor Meister $

32 Wood Rd., Braintree, MA, (781) 849-1970

www.konditormeister.com

Konditor Meister is a European-style bakery that's wedding central for any bride-to-be. Party supplies and tiered cakes line the window, and there's a cake tasting room in the back. These buttercream masters create an incredible variety of pastries, tarts, truffles, and petits fours. And their specialties are offered in individual servings from the dessert cases up front. Whether your pleasure is pecan tartlets or chocolate raspberry mousse cups, you can devour them on the spot or take them to a party. Chocolate-dipped strawberries are juicy and plump, and carrot cake muffins hide cream cheese icing in the center. Bite-sized cheesecakes and pastry swans filled with raspberry cream are the cherry on top.

THE GREATEST: **Muffins**

Gingerbread Construction Co. $

52 Main St., Wakefield, MA, (781) 246-2200

www.gingerbreadusa.com

Gingerbread Construction Co. builds ornamented gingerbread houses for any occasion, but they're best known for baking fabulous muffins in unusually good flavors. Their 19 flavors include chocolate chip, gingerbread with cream cheese icing, and chocolate raspberry topped with chocolate flakes and chocolate icing. The strawberry shortcake muffin is a summer specialty enveloping ripe fruit and whipped cream. But Phantom's absolute favorite is the Chocolate Dreme, which is made by injecting a moist chocolate muffin with chocolate cream. There's a second location in Winchester.

BBQ
GREAT ATE

THE GREATEST: Regional BBQ

RedBones $$

55 Chester Ave., Somerville, MA, (617) 628-2200

www.redbonesbbq.com

Covering the full sweep of the barbecue belt, RedBones has the best regional renditions of Texas beef, St. Louis ribs, and Georgia pulled pork. Tantalizing appetizers include the sausage of the day, hush puppies, Buffalo shrimp, and corn fritters. An eclectic crowd of bikers, families, and singles packs the psychedelic neon den downstairs, while barflies buzz about the bar upstairs, where 24 microbrews on tap change daily. Cyclists take note: RedBones offers a complimentary bicycle valet they say is the first of its kind in the nation.

THE GREATEST: Ribs

Uncle Pete's Hickory Ribs $$

72 Squire Rd., Revere, MA, (781) 289-7427

www.unclepetes.com

Uncle Pete's has the best ribs this side of the Mason-Dixon line. This meaty mecca is an unlikely intersection of Thai food and Southern BBQ. The wicked pork ribs are remarkably tender, thanks to a three-day cooking procedure that includes wood smoking over hickory, oak, and apple woods. The massive caramelized Texas beef ribs are steeped in rich spices, and the smoky pulled pork forgoes vinegar in favor of sweet BBQ sauce. Phantom also loves their Asian peanut slaw and the mango salsa served with fried tortillas.

THE GREATEST: BBQ Sandwiches

Blue Ribbon Bar-B-Q $

908 Massachusetts Ave., Arlington, MA, (781) 648-7427

www.blueribbonbbq.com

Blue Ribbon Bar-B-Q does Phantom's favorite BBQ-style sandwiches, full of pit-smoked specialties like Texas sliced beef brisket, Kansas City burnt ends, and Memphis dry-rubbed BBQ ribs. The oversized offerings come with baked beans, slaw, and homemade pickles. They'll even put together a feedbag for four or supper for six. Most customers blow through like tumbleweed, but the colorful chrome room done up with vintage signs and license plates makes eating in a lively option. There's a second Blue Ribbon in West Newton.

THE GREATEST: BBQ Sauce

Firefly's Bar-B-Que $$
350 E. Main St., Marlborough, MA, (508) 357-8883
www.fireflysbbq.com
Firefly's is a BBQ house where low and slow cooking is an art. Hickory, cherry, and apple woods smoke the meats, which are packed with intensity from dry spice rubs. For added flavor, the condiment bar includes five sauces (North or South Carolina, Memphis, spicy Beelzebar, Texas), assorted pickles, and 40 hot sauces. The best appetizer platter combines ribs, wings, brisket, catfish fingers, and homemade chips. And the grilled cracklin' bread is awesome topped with onions and smoked mozzarella.

THE GREATEST: Pulled Pork

Muddy River Smokehouse $$
21 Congress St., Portsmouth, NH, (603) 430-9582
www.muddyriver.com
Muddy River Smokehouse is a comfortable BBQ and Blues house where smoking, grilling, and saucing are taken very seriously. Their pulled pork, marinated in their delicious secret BBQ sauce, is incredibly tender thanks to 15 hours of slow smoking and hand shredding. Another highlight is the moist, flavorful ribs, rubbed with spices and then slow smoked over hickory logs for 12 hours. They also do baby back ribs, meaty St. Louis ribs, and the massive Texas rib nicknamed the "Fred Flintstone."

THE GREATEST: Bison BBQ

Bison County $$
275 Moody St., Waltham, MA, (781) 642-9720
www.bisoncounty.com
At Bison County, Texas and Southern-style BBQ are cooked on an eight-foot open grill in the middle of the dining room. They specialize in low-fat, low-cholesterol meat like bison burgers and grilled buffalo tips. But Phantom also enjoys the South Carolina wings, which are slow smoked and slathered with spicy mustard BBQ sauce. Order some sweet potato fries on the side. Thin slices and well-done crunchiness give them a familiar texture, but the natural sugars of the sweet potato add an irresistible flavor that the common spud can't match.

THE GREATEST: **Roadside BBQ**

M&M Ribs $

200 Geneva Ave., Dorchester, MA, (617) 306-0788

Working out of a converted box truck, M&M Ribs is a roadside eatery turning out incredible BBQ. The family-run operation is made up of three generations of barbecuers who are all named Moe. There's Big Moe, Little Moe, Tiny Moe, and No Moe. Their secret BBQ sauce is off the hook, but Phantom can't get past their beef and pork ribs. Whole chickens come barbecued or fried, and sides include BBQ beans, spicy rice, mac and cheese, collard greens, candied yams, potato salad, and coleslaw. For dessert, there's real peach cobbler and banana bread pudding.

THE GREATEST: **Mac and Cheese Bites**

Soul Fire Barbecue $$

182 Harvard Ave., Allston, MA, (617) 787-3003

www.soulfirebbq.com

"Serving all souls," Soul Fire Barbecue appeals to heat seekers with an appetite for brisket, pulled pork, and baby back ribs. The regional BBQ is pit smoked with a dry rub, and customers decide on the final slather from homemade sauces at the self-service BBQ bar. Choose from their signature Soul Fire Sauce, vinegar North Carolina hot sauce, South Carolina mustard sauce, and chili pepper Fiery Sauce. On the side, Southern fried mac and cheese bites are Phantom's dream appetizer come true. The crispy, crunchy nuggets are ooey-gooey inside, and they're irresistible dipped in molasses sweet sauce.

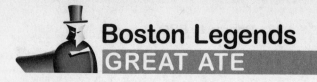

Boston Legends
GREAT ATE

THE GREATEST: JFK Lobster Stew

Locke-Ober $$$
3 Winter Pl., Boston, MA, (617) 542-1340
www.locke-ober.com

Locke-Ober has seen more marriage proposals than the Public Garden swan boats. Generations of Bostonians have dined here, including celebrities and high-profile politicians. The rich, buttery JFK lobster stew was renamed for its biggest fan, and the rest of the New England menu features creative fare like the pomegranate rack of lamb. The old-world setting is refined by dark mahogany and luxury leather. While the first and second floors are rich with history, the third is divided into six private chambers (the JFK room being the most prestigious) for intimate private parties and business meetings.

THE GREATEST: Sassy Service

Durgin-Park $$
340 Faneuil Hall Market Pl., Boston, MA, (617) 227-2038
www.durgin-park.com

Durgin-Park is a Boston institution with pack-'em-in feeding rooms crammed with communal checkered tables. Long-time customers make a regular pilgrimage for classic New England fare served at approachable prices. Hearty menu staples include clam chowder, Indian pudding, Boston baked beans, tons of seafood, cornbread, and Yankee pot roast. Sassy waitresses fall somewhere between witty and crass, but it's all in the name of good fun.

THE GREATEST: Seafood Chain

Legal Sea Foods $$$
14 Massachusetts locations
www.legalseafoods.com

A humongous list of 40 fishes makes Legal *the* homegrown seafood authority. Whether you're slurping creamy clam chowder solo at the bar or showing out-of-towners what New England is all about, it's a fun, happening place to be. The menu ranges from light lemon caper sole to wood-grilled scallops to nutty wild salmon. Guest chefs from places like China, the Caribbean, and India have spiced up the menu with exciting dishes like hot-and-sour seafood stew with jasmine rice. Massachusetts locations include the Prudential Center, Long Wharf, Chestnut Hill, and Park Square.

THE GREATEST: Greek Salad

Christo's $$
782 Crescent St., Brockton, MA, (508) 588-4200
Christo's built its legendary reputation on a world-famous Greek salad recipe. They start with crisp greens, cured olives, ripe tomatoes, and plenty of feta cheese. But, what sets Christo's apart is the homemade salad dressing that's so secret, even Phantom doesn't know all the ingredients. On the menu, you'll find other Hellenic favorites like juicy shish kebabs, baked lamb, crispy white pizza, and homemade baklava. Christo's has grown into a massive complex with five different dining rooms and a seasoned waitstaff that won't flinch when you ask for extra feta.

THE GREATEST: Roast Beef Sandwich

Kelly's Roast Beef $
410 Revere Beach Blvd., Revere Beach, MA, (781) 284-9129
www.kellysroastbeef.com
Revere beachgoers line up at Kelly's dozen takeout windows for the "original roast beef sandwich." Rosy Choice beef gets sliced thin and piled into a grilled poppy seed roll with super sloppy condiments like mayo and BBQ sauce. Somewhere between the sun, the sand, and the fearless seagulls, this local legend finds its fast food niche. The rest of the menu builds around a New England lineup of burgers, fried seafood, and quarter-pound lobster rolls. Additional locations include Danvers, Saugus, Natick, and Medford.

THE GREATEST: Inexpensive Italian

Galleria Umberto $
289 Hanover St., Boston, MA, (617) 227-5709
Galleria Umberto gets slammed at lunch, which is the only meal offered. The cafeteria-style eatery stays open until the food runs out, but you can call in your order to get a jump on the action. Although the menu is limited, you won't find better Sicilian specialties anywhere. Phantom arrives early for four kinds of calzones filled with combinations of ricotta, mozzarella, spinach, salami, and sausage. Square slices of Sicilian pizza come thick and cheesy, and deep-fried arancini rice balls hide pockets of peas and gravy. Every item costs next to nothing, including tiny Dixie cups of table wine.

THE GREATEST: Cannoli

Modern Pastry $
257 Hanover St., Boston, MA, (617) 523-3783
www.modernpastry.com

One of the North End's oldest pastry shops, Modern Pastry makes the best cannoli this side of the Boot. Crispy tubes of deep-fried pastry shell are filled at the last second so they don't get soggy, and then dipped in chocolate or almonds. Other Italian specialties include colorful Italian cookies, and almond marzipan shaped into peaches, watermelon, and cherries. Modern makes masterful ricotta pie and specialty cakes, and they're so fast at wrapping up your order, you'll be out of there before you can say cappuccino. There's a second location in Medford.

THE GREATEST: Historic Landmark

Union Oyster House $$
41 Union St., Boston, MA, (617) 227-2750
www.unionoysterhouse.com

Union Oyster House near Boston's famous Faneuil Hall is America's oldest restaurant, so of course, it's mobbed by tourists. Phantom says, skip the overpriced entrées and slip into the cozy oyster bar instead, where Daniel Webster ate every day. It's curved like a horseshoe and small enough to get lots of attention from expert shuckers slicing littlenecks and cherrystones to order. If you're hungry for more, they have lobsters at up to ten whopping pounds. The rest of the wood-beam rooms are filled with glass lanterns and old historical photos. Be sure to stop by the famous Kennedy Booth, which was always reserved for JFK.

Breakfast
GREAT ATE

THE GREATEST: Bargain Breakfast

Brookline Lunch $
9 Brookline St., Cambridge, MA, (617) 354-2983
Ironically, Brookline Lunch is Phantom's favorite place to get breakfast in Cambridge. There's no better bargain than their dirt-cheap eggs and fluffy pancakes. Every omelet is piled high with skillet home fries and grilled veggies and comes with hot sauce, toast, and homemade jam. The small nook is big on charm, with weathered paint and a mishmash of cheery colors splashed from the open kitchen to the tall wooden booths. Lunch offers a glimpse of the owners' Middle Eastern heritage with kebabs, creamy hummus, crispy falafel, and stuffed grape leaves.

THE GREATEST: Breakfast Menu

Persy's Place $$
35 Main St., Plymouth, MA, (508) 732-9876
Specializing in hearty Yankee fare, Persy's Place boasts the biggest breakfast menu Phantom has ever seen. Most plates come with Boston baked beans and grilled corn bread, and range from corned beef hash to Belgian waffles made with bacon in the batter. The astounding variety includes biscuits and gravy, and chocolate chip–banana buttermilk pancakes. Crepes, lobster omelets, and an amazing Monte Cristo ham sandwich on French toast round out the offerings. Locations include Hyannis, Dartmouth, Mashpee, and Middleboro.

THE GREATEST: Cafeteria-Style

The Paramount $$
44 Charles St., Boston, MA, (617) 720-1152
www.paramountboston.com
The Paramount has the best breakfast in Beacon Hill. The coffee shop atmosphere is inviting, and cafeteria-style service keeps it cheap. The open-griddle kitchen does simple stuff right: bacon and eggs, and bagel sandwiches stuffed with sausage, egg, and cheese. Feta spinach omelets come with toast and home fries, and the malted Belgian waffles are topped with fresh fruit. The lunch menu turns to burgers and amazing grilled cheese, and dinner switches gears as they dim the lights and offer full service.

THE GREATEST: Blueberry Pancakes

Mike's City Diner $
1714 Washington St., Boston, MA, (617) 267-9393
Mike's City Diner is an old-school luncheonette serving the city's best American breakfast. Staples include blueberry pancakes, linguica omelets, and Belgian waffles smothered in whipped cream and strawberries. Big appetites order the "Emergency Room" special of two eggs, two pancakes, bacon, grits, and toast. But Phantom prefers the "Intensive Care" unit of three eggs and a 10-ounce sirloin steak. Mike's is one of the few places you can get an omelet folded over corned beef hash or corned beef, and their cinnamon walnut waffles are almost as sweet as the apple pie.

THE GREATEST: Belgian Waffles

Sound Bites $
708 Broadway, Somerville, MA, (617) 623-8338
Sound Bites may be a hole in the wall with pushy service, long lines, and a "no newspapers" rule, but Phantom can't resist their Belgian waffles. Whole-grain squares are topped with whipped cream and a mountain of exotic fresh fruit like papaya, kiwi, blueberries, strawberries, banana, and mango. Additional standouts include grilled blueberry muffins and omelets like the Art, Tom, and Jack filled with artichokes, tomatoes, and jack cheese. Their unbelievable "NoPlaceLikeHomeFries" are basically a brick of fried garlic mashed potatoes. While waiting for a table, customers serve themselves at the coffee bar.

THE GREATEST: 24-Hour Breakfast

Friendly Toast $$
121 Congress St., Portsmouth, NH, (603) 430-2154
Open 24 hours on weekends, Friendly Toast is an all-time breakfast favorite. The eclectic eatery is full of flea market finds, '50s kitsch, and the best collection of bad art north of Manhattan's East Village. It's a funky feast for both the eyes and the stomach, serving greasy spoon goodies with a sophisticated twist. Phantom is nuts about the Almond Joy Pancakes and the Green Eggs and Ham on anadama toast. The huge menu also includes dinner fare like sweet potato Orleans fries covered in a sweet-spicy-messy mix of brown sugar, Tabasco, and sour cream.

THE GREATEST: **Pastrami Scramble**

Johnny's Luncheonette $
30 Langley Rd., Newton, MA, (617) 527-3223
www.johnnysluncheonette.com
A '50s-style eatery with a '90s twist, Johnny's Luncheonette is a fun diner filled
with big booths and counter stools. Soda-fountain frappes are appropriate at any
hour, and breakfast is served straight through dinner. The huge menu specializes in
creative comfort food like the three-egg pastrami scramble with caramelized onions
and homemade turkey apple sausage. The corn-bread-crusted French toast is made
from thick-sliced challah and toasted almonds, and crunchy granola French toast is
even sweeter with pure maple syrup.

THE GREATEST: **French Toast**

Zaftigs $$
335 Harvard St., Brookline, MA, (617) 975-0075
www.zaftigs.com
Zaftigs specializes in guilty pleasure plates in the a.m. This creative deli serves the
most decadent French toast Phantom has ever eaten. Their gooey banana-stuffed
version is made with bourbon-vanilla batter and accompanied by sweet date butter.
Other temptations include cheddar apple omelets, cheese blintzes smothered in
sour cream, and fresh bagels loaded with cream cheese and lox. Later in the day, in-
dulge in hot brisket over potato pancakes or chicken matzo ball soup like your Jew-
ish mother makes.

Brunch
GREAT ATE

THE GREATEST: **Bloody Mary Bar**

East Coast Grill & Raw Bar $$
1271 Cambridge St., Cambridge, MA, (617) 491-6568
www.eastcoastgrill.net
East Coast Grill & Raw Bar is a famously fun restaurant with a wacky Sunday
brunch that claims the world's largest Bloody Mary bar. It's a make-your-own
smorgasbord including three tomato bases, a half-dozen spices from curry to pa-
prika, a dozen hot sauces, skewered fruit and olives, and inventive sauces like
mango-habanero. Chef-owner Chris Schlesinger puts out a bold Latin-inspired
brunch that includes their signature barbecued seafood. Steak and eggs comes with
pickled peppers and fried sweet potatoes, and there's an awesome omelet with avo-
cado, black beans, cheese, and guava. Phantom always tacks on an order of Mon-
terey jack grits with pineapple, bacon, and plantains.

THE GREATEST: **Saturday Brunch**

Harvard Gardens $$
316 Cambridge St., Boston, MA, (617) 523-2727
www.harvardgardens.com
Harvard Gardens serves Phantom's favorite Sunday *and* Saturday brunch until
3 p.m., specializing in modern comfort food. The same stylish crew crowding the
handsome bar the night before pops back in for applewood-smoked bacon, chocolate and banana stuffed French toast, and HG Eggs Benny stacked with smoked
salmon. Most plates include a croissant, and you can add on an order of crispy
"Damn Good Home Fries" infused with Parmesan and sautéed onions. The space
oozes class, from the hardwood floors to the sleek banquettes.

THE GREATEST: **Jazz Brunch**

Red Rock Bistro $$
141 Humphrey St., Swampscott, MA, (781) 595-1414
www.redrockbistro.com
If you're brunching on the North Shore, it had better be at Red Rock Bistro. Live
jazz sets the mood, and diners get a clear shot of the Boston skyline across the bay.
Creative American classics include Belgian waffles with Vermont maple syrup,

steak and eggs smothered in hollandaise, and fried eggs served over sweet potato and chorizo hash. Brunch is half lunch, so you can also score Red Rock's signature: fried clams piled into a brown paper bag with tartar on the side. Their other paper bag creation is fresh donuts plated with mango yogurt for dipping.

THE GREATEST: Huevos Rancheros

Metropolis Café $
584 Tremont St., Boston, MA, (617) 247-2931
Metropolis Café is a tiny tin of a neighborhood restaurant with one of the city's best brunches. Served on Saturday and Sunday, the memorable meal includes grapefruit mimosas, Boursin and chive omelets, and apple-chicken sausage. The banana pancakes are spectacular, the creamy grits come with chorizo and fried eggs, and the huevos rancheros are balanced over cumin black bean hash. Customers squeeze into the tightly spaced tables and read the paper at the wrap-around bar.

THE GREATEST: Champagne Brunch

Foxwoods Sunday Champagne Brunch $$$
Great Cedar Hotel, 39 Norwich-Westerly Road, Ledyard, CT,
(800) 369-9663
www.foxwoods.com
When Phantom heads to "The Woods" for the weekend, the only sure bet is the Sunday Champagne Brunch in the Sunset Ballroom. Ice sculptures and chocolate fountains are highlights, but it's the sprawling buffet that keeps the Caped Critic coming back for more . . . and more . . . and more. It's so expansive, you almost need a golf cart to get around. As the name implies, there's champagne toast included, along with coffee and endless juice. The insane brunch spread will have you juggling pastries, a sushi station, carved meats, seafood like oysters and shrimp cocktail, pasta, made-to-order omelets and crepes, and desserts.

THE GREATEST: Pajama Brunch

Tremont 647 $$
647 Tremont St., Boston, MA, (617) 266-4600
www.tremont647.com
Tremont 647 is known for its unusually delicious food, but every Saturday and Sunday the stylish space transforms into a fun pajama brunch. Customers and servers roll out of bed and sport their sleepwear right into the dining room. The daring menu dishes out chocolate chip pancakes, breakfast pizza, and Andy's signature MoMos (pork-ginger dumplings). There's croissant French toast and lobster

and grits with poached eggs. Some waitresses have been known to get a little risqué with their bedtime attire, and there have been reports of a certain large someone in purple silk PJs.

THE GREATEST: **Gourmet Buffet**

Henrietta's Table $$$
The Charles Hotel, 1 Bennett St., Cambridge, MA, (617) 661-5005
www.henriettastable.com

Henrietta's Table is an upscale country kitchen with a spectacular Sunday brunch at a spectacularly expensive price. From noon to 3 p.m., it's an all-you-can-eat feast of fresh-shucked Wellfleet oysters, bacon, sausage, and smoked fish. They have three hot entrées, an omelet station, and crispy waffles. Fresh-squeezed orange juice flows like water, and you don't have to finish your farm fresh eggs before hitting the 10-dessert smorgasbord. The rustic dining room is so homey, you can dress up or just throw on a pair of jeans.

THE GREATEST: **Breakfast Bargain**

Neighborhood Restaurant & Bakery $
25 Bow St., Somerville, MA, (617) 628-2151
www.neighborhoodrestaurantandbakery.com

Neighborhood Restaurant & Bakery is one of the best bargain brunches around. Every heaping plate comes with unlimited coffee or tea, a small orange juice, home fries, homemade pastries, and a choice of fresh fruit or hot cereal. The menu is home-style American with a Portuguese twist that often includes linguica sausage. They have cheesy omelets, tropical papaya pancakes, and sweet French toast served with three eggs, any style. Fun colors brighten the walls, and in the summer the driveway offers outdoor seating with a vine-covered trellis overhead.

Burgers
GREAT ATE

THE GREATEST: **Burger Selection**

Bartley's Burger Cottage $
1246 Massachusetts Ave., Cambridge, MA, (617) 354-6559
www.mrbartley.com

Bartley's Burger Cottage is practically an extension of the Harvard campus with its dormlike décor, plastic patio seating, and student-friendly prices. They get crazy creative with celebrity-named burgers. The Tiger Woods is above par with cheddar and guacamole. The Stephen King is a monster/Muenster cheeseburger with coleslaw and fries. And the Arnold Schwarzenegger double-Swiss cheeseburger is jacked up on 14 ounces of beef. Cajun sweet potato fries are a required course, not an elective. To graduate, enjoy candy frappes flavored with Peppermint Patties, Snickers, M&Ms, or Reese's Peanut Butter Cups.

THE GREATEST: **20-Minute Burger**

R. F. O'Sullivan's Pub $
282 Beacon St., Somerville, MA, (617) 492-7773
www.rfosullivan.com

Phantom heads to O'Sullivan's for thick, juicy, mouth-watering burgers. Each belly-busting beast is a half-pound of ground sirloin that requires 20 minutes on the grill and comes with hand-cut steak fries. O'Sullivans is one of the only restaurants that will serve a burger the way Phantom likes it—RARE! The menu lists two dozen versions like the Black & Blue coated in fresh ground pepper and topped with blue cheese. The House burger is decked out in ham and bacon, and the Cape Codder lights up with avocado and Swiss. Or skip the carbs altogether and order the Bunless burger on a garden salad, all smothered in sautéed peppers and onions.

THE GREATEST: **Double Cheeseburger**

UBURGER $
636 Beacon St., Boston, MA, (617) 536-0448

UBURGER is a sizzling fast food joint that refuses to compromise on quality. Everything is made from scratch and to order, from the onion rings and hand-cut shoestring fries to the quarter-pound patties. Absolutely no heat lamps are allowed, and you can pimp your burger out with two dozen toppings. Specialties include the

Cowboy Burger topped with BBQ sauce, jack cheese, sautéed mushrooms, and crispy bacon; the Boom Burger, fired up with spicy chipotle sauce; and the Stunt Double Cheeseburger with jalapeños and banana peppers, for daredevils only.

THE GREATEST: Toppings

Fuddruckers $
Saugus, Reading, and North Andover locations
www.fuddruckersNE.com
At Fuddruckers, burgers come in four different-sized patties as large as a pound. But hey, size doesn't matter. It's the toppings that make these burgers special. There's a complimentary produce bar loaded with everything from lettuce and tomatoes to nacho cheese, salsa, and jalapeños. Smoked bacon, homemade chili, and guacamole are a little extra. The house-baked buns are fluffy, buttery, and just plain awesome. After throwing back a coffee, mocha, or Oreo shake, and a bowling ball-sized burger, you can't leave Fuddruckers hungry.

THE GREATEST: Mini Burgers

Match $$
94 Massachusetts Ave., Boston, MA, (617) 247-9922
www.matchbackbay.com
As a trendy hot spot, Match offers the coolest comfort food around. Martinis and mini-burgers pair perfectly as you sink into the swank setting and enjoy the 14-foot fireplace. The three-ounce sliders are just right for snacking, but they come in so many flavors, you can mix-and-match a meal. Beyond the basic cheeseburger, there's are veggie, chicken, lamb, and even lobster burgers available. The sausage burger comes with sweet onions, and the soy and ginger-marinated tuna burger is slicked with wasabi aioli. Since they're so small, you'll still have room for desserts like the pan-seared cookie dough or the caramelized banana split.

THE GREATEST: Japanese-Style Burger

Café Mami $
1815 Massachusetts Ave., Cambridge, MA, (617) 547-9130
Located in the Porter Exchange Asian food court, Café Mami puts a Japanese twist on the all-American hamburger. They're called "hamburg steak sets," and they don't come on a bun. Each hand-packed patty slides onto the plate with a side salad and all the rice you can eat. Customers get a choice of homemade sauces like sweet teriyaki or rich tomato sauce that's been simmering for a full day. Add melted mozzarella for a Japanese-style cheeseburger, or top it Phantom's favorite way, with a runny fried egg.

THE GREATEST: **Angus Beef Patties**

Wild Willy's $
46 Arsenal St., Watertown, MA, (617) 926-9700
www.wildwillysburgers.com
Wild Willy's is a cowboy-themed burger joint filled with 10-gallon hats, spurs, and
painted landscapes of the West. Customers sidle up to the counter and order a big
ol' charbroiled Angus burger on a buttery grilled bun. The tangy Bubba Burger
wears BBQ sauce, crispy bacon, pickles, onion, and cheddar, while the Rio Grande
includes roasted green chiles from New Mexico. Sweet frappes and floats finish off
the feast. The York, Maine, location shows off a talking mechanical cowboy, and
there's a third Wild Willy's in Rochester, New Hampshire.

THE GREATEST: **Brioche Buns**

Flat Patties $
81 Mt. Auburn St., Cambridge, MA, (617) 871-6871
Tucked away in the Garage food court, Flat Patties focuses on fresh-ground,
quarter-pound burgers. They're grilled to order and served on light, airy brioche
buns at ridiculously low prices. On the side, order crispy onion rings, hand-cut
French fries, or the ultimate chili cheese fries. Their other specialty is all-American
sandwiches like grilled chicken or pulled pork. The owner's favorite is the rare
roast beef sandwich smothered in BBQ sauce, horseradish, or mayo. For something
spicier, head around the corner and down the stairs to Felipe's Taqueria.

Chain
GREAT ATE

THE GREATEST: Bloomin' Onion

Outback Steakhouse $$
670 locations
www.outback.com
Outback Steakhouse is the birthplace of the Bloomin' Onion, and no imitator comes close. This batter-fried "Aussie-Tizer" is crunchy, spicy, and addictive, and it simmers down with a creamy dipping sauce. Outback is dependable for flavorful steaks and features fun Aussie-inspired menu names like Kookaburra wings. Plus, you can add shrimp from the barbie to any entrée. Other Outback favorites include crackly Gold Coast Coconut Shrimp and cheese fries smothered in massive amounts of Monterey jack, cheddar, and bacon. Call-ahead seating and curbside take-away make the Outback an unbeatable Down Under deal.

THE GREATEST: Rolls

Bertucci's $$
40 Massachusetts locations
www.bertuccis.com
Bertucci's makes amazing brick-oven pizza, but Phantom could make a meal out of their hot breadbasket alone. Their signature rolls are soft, crusty, and baked fresh every hour. They come with olive oil dipping sauce spiked with red pepper flakes, garlic, and parsley. The light, crackly pizzas slide out of an 850-degree oven in the open kitchen. Creative toppings are worked into combos like the Mediterranean pie with rosemary, sage, and sun-dried tomatoes. There's also a grilled chicken and broccoli pie with lemon pepper cream sauce. Request a complimentary ball of dough for your kids to mold so you can sit back and relax.

THE GREATEST: Shakes

Johnny Rockets $
175 locations
www.johnnyrockets.com
Johnny Rockets is a '50s-themed diner chain with a real soda bar where you might expect to see the Fonz. It's where Phantom stops for creamy hand-dipped shakes. Every order includes a backup serving in a metal mixer cup. It's like two shakes for

the price of one! The all-American menu features retro hamburgers formed from one-third-pound patties. They're hand pressed, grilled, and topped with cheddar, mushrooms, onions, and bacon. Chili fries make a fine side and, for dessert, Johnny Rockets serves hot apple pie. Soda jerks bop around in bowties and little white caps, singing and dancing to the oldies with ketchup bottle "mics."

THE GREATEST: Lettuce Wraps

P. F. Chang's $$
8 Park Plaza, Boston, MA, (617) 573-0821
www.pfchangs.com

P. F. Chang's has successfully transplanted Chinese food into a hip, contemporary chain. Phantom would go for the lettuce wraps alone; bits of garlicky chicken and crispy noodles come with a side of crisp iceberg "cups" so you can assemble the hot and cold appetizer yourself. The menu includes spicy orange peel beef and ginger chicken with broccoli. For desserts, do not attempt the six-layer Great Wall of Chocolate alone. With servers whipping up sauces tableside and Mongolian warrior sculptures all around, Chang's is a popular place for birthday dinners.

THE GREATEST: Sandwiches

Panera Bread $
773 locations
www.panera.com

Panera Bread is a perky lunch place, and it's the best sandwich chain around. Create your own on handcrafted artisanal breads like honey wheat, rosemary walnut, and kalamata olive bread. Or choose from top sellers like the pesto Tuscan chicken on rosemary focaccia. Phantom's favorites are the roast beef with creamy horseradish sauce on an Asiago demi-loaf, and the Bacon Turkey Bravo on tomato basil bread. Hot soups like chicken noodle and broccoli cheddar can be ladled into fresh bread bowls, and there are creative salads, too. Going above and beyond, Panera offers fireplaces and free Wi-Fi access.

THE GREATEST: Spinach Artichoke Dip

Houston's $$$
60 State St., Boston, MA, (617) 573-9777
www.houstons.com

Houston's is almost too trendy to be a chain. The four-sided bar is always packed, and the tiered dining room features red leather booths. The most delicious thing on the menu is the garlicky Chicago-style spinach dip: served creamy-thick with warm tortilla chips, salsa, and sour cream, it's one addictive appetizer. The menu ranges from cedar plank salmon to ribs and french fries. And for an exciting Asian dish, try the Evil Jungle Thai Steak Salad studded with avocado, basil, mango, and peanuts. Desserts like the cappuccino five-nut brownie make quite a splash, too.

THE GREATEST: Side Dishes

Boston Market $
27 Massachusetts locations
www.bostonmarket.com

Boston Market turns out quite a selection of side dishes. Best of all, they're on display, reducing the surprise factor so common with fast food. The mac and cheese is a gooey trifecta of American, cheddar, and blue cheese. Mashed potatoes and stuffing are classic go-to sides, but you can spice things up with the sweet potato casserole, garlic dill potatoes, or hot cinnamon apples. Make a meal out of the home-style veggies or pair them with a Chicken Carver sandwich smeared with creamy Dijon. The rotisserie chickens are surprisingly juicy for a chain, basting in their own juices as they turn over the flames.

THE GREATEST: Fruit Bouquet

Edible Arrangements $$$
300 locations
www.ediblearrangements.com

Cross a bouquet of flowers with a bowl of fruit, and you get the hottest new idea in gift giving. Edible Arrangements improves on the traditional produce basket by sculpting skewered fruit into intricate floral arrangements. Phantom loves the bouquet of chocolate-dipped strawberries. The signature Delicious Fruit Design incorporates pineapple "daisies," cantaloupe, honeydew, strawberries, and grapes. Customers can add fudge dipping sauce, balloons, or a teddy bear. Walk-in customers are welcome, but most orders are taken in advance and delivered by refrigerated van.

Local Chains
GREAT ATE

THE GREATEST: **Upscale Pizza Chain**

Figs   **$$**
Locations in Charlestown and Beacon Hill
www.toddenglish.com
The Figs chain is Todd English's cross between a European bistro and a pizzeria.
Servers in jeans and T-shirts deliver Italian entrées, and thin-crust pizza is the sig-
nature item. Propped on an upside-down cookie sheet, the free-form pizza pies are
crispy with boldly flavored toppings. Phantom favors the sauceless bianco piled
with caramelized onions and balsamic drizzled arugula. The fig-and-prosciutto pie
has a rosemary crust; the spicy shrimp is topped with avocado and tomato relish;
and the Italian sausage pizza includes charred eggplant and torn basil.

THE GREATEST: **Family-Style**

Vinny T's   **$$**
8 Massachusetts locations
www.vinnytsofboston.com
Okay, Vinnie T's isn't that great, but they serve everything in huge family-style
platters with red sauce classics that everybody loves. Phantom rounds up his big-
bellied friends to pass around platters of fried calamari, lasagna, fettuccine carbonara, penne alla vodka, and veal marsala. Appetizers and entrées come in two
sizes, and parties of six can opt for the four-course prix fixe. The atmosphere is
boisterous, packed with people and pictures of famous Italian Americans. No one
leaves hungry or empty-handed!

THE GREATEST: **Bagel Chain**

Finagle A Bagel
19 Massachusetts locations
www.finagleabagel.com
The "Bagel Buzz Saw" gets a lot of attention, but it's the tasty bagels themselves
that make an impression at Finagle A Bagel. Every step of the bagel-making process is done in full view of the customers, from boiling and baking the dough to
cooling and preparing the final product. The 17 varieties include plain, onion,
poppy, apple caramel, triple chocolate chip, and jalapeño cheddar. Upgrade your

27

bagel to a sandwich like the smoked house club with bacon and chipotle mayo. Or top it with smoked salmon and scallion cream cheese.

THE GREATEST: Cape Cod Cooking

Hearth 'n Kettle $
7 Massachusetts locations
www.hearthnkettle.com

Located along the main streets of Cape Cod and Southeastern Massachusetts, Hearth 'n Kettle serves three affordable meals a day with straightforward simplicity. The rustic dining rooms feature wooden beams, high-backed booths, and working fireplaces. For lunch and dinner, their mantra is "Cape Cod Fresh," as the kitchen utilizes local seafood and dayboat haddock and sea scallops. Phantom's favorite meal at the H 'n K is breakfast, for their hot-out-of-the-oven breads, muffins, and pastries. For a true taste of the Cape, try the thick sweet potato and cranberry pancakes with walnuts.

THE GREATEST: Trendy Chain

RooBar $$
586 Main St., Hyannis, MA, (508) 778-6515
www.theroobar.com

When you want to escape the Cape without leaving the peninsula, RooBar is the perfect place. Nothing about it screams flip-flops and lobster print pants, so be sure to pack your weekend bag full of clubbing gear. All four locations (Chatham, Falmouth, and Plymouth, too) are sleek and sexy with urban atmosphere. But each one pioneers its own trendy menu. Adventurous eaters enjoy crazy concoctions like cinnamon steak, tuna parfait with cilantro lime sorbet, banana encrusted halibut, and soy-candied spiced ribs. RooBar also does outstanding pizzas with toppings like duck confit, spiced lamb, or a balsamic glaze.

THE GREATEST: Chicken Wing Chain

Wings Over Brookline $
477 Harvard St., Brookline, MA, (617) 264-WING (9464)
www.wingsoverbrookline.com

Wings Over Brookline is part of a chicken chain that's flying into college towns across the Northeast. Business is mostly takeout, but eat-in diners can put their taste buds on autopilot in the aviation-themed storefront. The guilty-pleasures menu targets late-night cravings with 22 flavors of hand-battered chicken wings, all available in boneless or bone-in versions. Along with five heat levels from Wimpy to After Burner, there are offbeat sauces like Mustang Ranch, Honey Lime, and

Lemon Pepper. West Texas Mesquite tastes as addictive as BBQ potato chips, and Garlic Parmesan is incredibly crunchy. Burgers and St. Louis–style ribs round out the menu. Delivery runs seven days a week until 2 a.m.

THE GREATEST: Big Apple Pancake

Bickfords Grille $
27 Massachusetts locations
www.bickfords.com
Bickford's Grille is the local answer to IHOP. Flapjack favorites include the Strawberry Supreme Pancakes and the Big Apple Pancake oozing cinnamon sugar. Lobster omelets and steak and eggs are standouts, too. New England comfort food continues into lunch and dinner, with specialties like creamy clam chowder, lobster rolls overflowing with knuckle and claw meat, and roasted turkey served with stuffing and giblet gravy. The Ipswich clam dinner compiles fresh fried whole bellies, and the Yankee pot roast is so darn tender, you won't need a knife to cut it.

THE GREATEST: Fast, Hot, Affordable Lunch

Viga $$
3 Boston locations
www.vigaeatery.com
Viga is one of Boston's best lunch spots, with Downtown locations on Devonshire and Pearl streets and a third on Stuart Street in the Back Bay. Once inside, customers push toward a station and yell out their order. In a matter of seconds, hot Italian fare like pasta, calzones, and eggplant Parm are good to go. Their New York–style pizza is ready-to-heat in enormous slices that are bigger than Phantom's head. Sandwiches come on grilled focaccia, which is also cut into breadsticks and offered as a free snack while you wait. Cookies and cakes are piled around the checkout register, with unusual treasures like Fruit Loops cereal squares.

Chinese
GREAT ATE

THE GREATEST: **Upscale Chinese**

Golden Temple $$$
1651 Beacon St., Brookline, MA, (617) 277-9722
When Phantom craves fine Chinese food and the strongest Mai Tai on the eastern seaboard, he heads for "The Temple." It's one of the area's most beautiful restaurants, combining a modern mix of architecture, lighting, and music. The high-end cuisine comes at a price, but luxurious dishes like Chardonnay chicken and batter-fried lobster are worth a few extra bucks. The Brookline institution is always innovating, and the bar scene sizzles at night with a house DJ and dancing.

THE GREATEST: **Food Court Alternative**

Bernard's $$
Chestnut Hill Mall, 199 Boylston St., Chestnut Hill, MA, (617) 969-3388
Bernard's is a delightful stir-fried surprise in the Chestnut Hill Mall. This unlikely location is no indication of the spectacular food and excellent service inside. The dining room is decked out in bamboo shades and features a jade colored wall etched in jungle scenes. It's always full of regulars who come for the tempting menu of Chinese, pan-Asian, and healthy "spa" selections. Phantom's purple chopsticks head straight for the sautéed shrimp with roasted black beans or the grilled sirloin steak over steamed jade broccoli.

THE GREATEST: **Chinese and Sushi**

Billy Tse $$
240 Commercial St., Boston, MA, (617) 227-9990
www.billytesrestaurant.com
What's a Pan-Asian restaurant doing in Boston's Italian North End? Serving some of the most sophisticated Chinese and Japanese cuisine around! Billy Tse brings a sense of style to the modern atmosphere and offers surprisingly light cuisine. Businessmen and neighborhood residents pack the bar, the dining room, and the sushi bar. Phantom chooses the sesame chicken, Taipei fried rice, and coconut shrimp; and it's too tempting to pass on sushi rolls like the East maki with shrimp, avocado, and cucumber. The original Billy Tse is in Revere.

THE GREATEST: **Spare Ribs**

Chinatown $$
103 Sharon St., Stoughton, MA, (781) 297-3886
Residents of the South Shore need not venture all the way to Boston's Chinatown when their very own Chinatown serves authentic Asian food in Stoughton and Brockton. The massive kitchen is visible from the dining room through glass walls, and one glimpse of the master chefs proves these guys know how to work a wok. The Chicken Scrolls have moist meat inside every crunchy bite. The regular spare ribs are delicious. But for the ultimate appetizer, the meaty Chinatown special ribs are even bigger with the same sweet, succulent flavor.

THE GREATEST: **Ultimate Asian Complex**

Kowloon $$
948 Broadway, Saugus, MA, (781) 233-0077
www.kowloonrestaurant.com
It's almost impossible to describe the Kowloon to anyone who has never experienced this Asian food and entertainment complex. Owned and operated by the Wong family since 1950, the Kowloon has evolved into a landmark on Route 1 in Saugus. With seating for nearly 1,200 customers, it's a mind-bogglingly large operation featuring Chinese food, a Thai kitchen, a sushi bar, and the Comedy Connection comedy club. Phantom's favorite dishes include garlicky Saugus Wings, chicken and shrimp lo mein, and lobster with ginger and scallions.

THE GREATEST: **Late-Night Lounge**

Peking Tom's $$
25 Kingston St., Boston, MA, (617) 482-6282
www.pekingtom.com
Bringing a nostalgic twist to Boston's cool cocktail crowd, Peking Tom's Longtang Lounge is as fun as it is funky. The hip bar mixes a colorful list of adult beverages like Fog Cutters, Mai Tais, and Scorpion Bowls. The food is abundant and easy to share, with specialties including seafood Peking dumplings, Szechuan salt and pepper squid, and kung pao chicken lettuce wraps. Peking Tom's is always jumping after work and after hours, when festive dining and imbibing kicks into high gear.

THE GREATEST: Pu Pu Platters

Quan's Kitchen $$

652 East Washington St., North Attleboro, MA, (508) 699-7826

www.quanskitchen.net

Located in a strip mall, Quan's Kitchen is a completely unexpected delight. The stylish, modern interior sports ruby red walls and sleek light fixtures. Even the pu pu platters have personality. Instead of a flaming presentation on a wooden tray, the boneless spare ribs, egg rolls, and beef teriyaki are laid out geometrically on a white porcelain platter. General Gau himself would go to war over their rendition of the sweet and spicy recipe, and the sushi chefs slice and dice in full view of the dining room. Quan has a second (takeout and delivery only) kitchen in Mansfield.

THE GREATEST: Yakitori Bar

Ginseng Restaurant & Lounge $

220 Worcester Rd., Framingham, MA, (508) 620-0102

www.ginsengframingham.com

Ginseng is an Asian emporium hosting New England's only yakitori bar. With seats that look through a glass wall and directly into the kitchen, it's not just dinner, it's dinner theater. Skewered snacks like tender chicken, bacon-wrapped asparagus, juicy scallops, shrimp, lamb chops, and eggplant are cooked over an open grill and served steaming hot. The rest of the menu spans Southeast Asia with everything from Peking dumplings and lettuce wraps to fried chicken with fresh watermelon and Thai-style spare ribs.

Comfort Food
GREAT ATE

THE GREATEST: Chicken Soup

New England Soup Factory $
2 Brookline Place, Brookline, MA, (617) 739-1695
www.nesoupfactory.com
With only a half-dozen tables, New England Soup Factory is ideal for takeout. The
rotating menu changes daily, featuring 10 of their made-from-scratch soups. The
triple-strength chicken vegetable stocks a robust broth full of white meat morsels
and tender carrots. Other slurpable standouts include sweet potato soup with
caramelized onions, lobster Newburg, and clam and corn chowder. Customers who
can't decide are encouraged to sample from the simmering assortment. Iced soups
are served in warmer months, but you can always order overstuffed sandwiches,
salads, brownies, blondies, and cookies. There's a second location in Newton.

THE GREATEST: Hot Chocolate

L. A. Burdick Chocolate $
52-D Brattle St., Cambridge, MA, (617) 491-4340
www.burdickchocolate.com
Burdick Chocolate is a cozy European-style café turning out the most delicious
chocolate treats. Their hot chocolate is hands-down the best Phantom has ever had!
Poured into a giant mug, the rich drink is like a liquefied candy bar mixed with
steamed milk. Still, it's not too sweet. Their adorable chocolate mice are almost too
cute to eat, constructed with a ganache body, almond ears, and a ribbon tail. Other
treats include dessert cakes, fruit tartlets, and tea cookies. Burdick's flagship location is in Walpole, New Hampshire.

THE GREATEST: Steak Sauces

Vintage $$$
1430 VFW Pkwy. (Bridge St.), West Roxbury, MA, (617) 469-2600
www.vintagerestaurants.com
It may be called Vintage, but this dark wood steakhouse has a trendy atmosphere.
Modern meat eaters can count on a choice chophouse menu featuring tender filet
mignon. But it's the special sauces that give the kitchen a voice of its own. Along
with the expected béarnaise and merlot demi-glaze, they up the sauce ante with

port-fig demi-glaze, citrus soy ginger sauce, lemon caper beurre blanc, and Cajun jalapeño butter. For a little extra, you can top your rib eye or New York strip with melted blue cheese or lobster cream sauce. Inventive entrées include the stuffed pork loin rolled around apple breading. Vintage is a bit south of the city, but you can't beat the complimentary valet.

THE GREATEST: Chicken Pie

Harrow's Chicken Pie $
126 Main St., Reading, MA, (781) 944-0410
www.chickenpie.com

Harrow's Chicken Pie has a phenomenal 60-year-old recipe for their namesake specialty. What was once a full-service restaurant is now strictly a takeout business. The cars line up for soul-satisfying pies packed with huge chunks of chicken, homemade gravy, carrots, and potatoes in a golden, freshly baked crust. They're available in four sizes that range from individual portions to the mammoth six-person pie. These all-natural delicacies are available hot or cold, along with mashed potatoes and veggie sides. Phantom likes to order extra chicken gravy and then follow through with blueberry pie for dessert.

THE GREATEST: Sizzling Steak

Frank's Steakhouse $$
2310 Massachusetts Ave., Cambridge, MA, (617) 661-0666
www.frankssteakhouse.com

Frank's Steakhouse is famous for multiple reasons, but Phantom can't get past their Famous New York Sizzler Sirloin. They aren't kidding with this dish: it's practically on fire when it comes out of the kitchen on a cast-iron skillet. Frank's is also the oldest steakhouse in all of Greater Boston, established way back in 1938. If you're a meat-and-potatoes kind of guy like the Caped Critic, you'll love the old-school menu filled with burgers, pasta, and affordable pub grub. They also offer a deep-fried onion loaf inspired by Norm on *Cheers*. With a casual atmosphere and a piano bar packed with locals, this neighborhood place is just right for families.

THE GREATEST: Fondue

The Wine Cellar $$$
30 Massachusetts Ave., Boston, MA, (617) 236-0080
www.bostoncellar.com

The Wine Cellar in the Back Bay makes it possible to dip into fondue for your appetizer, your entrées, and your dessert. They offer more than 20 delicious fondues, divided into cheese, oil-based, and sweet categories. Beyond the basics, they offer intriguing fondues like the Cheddar Melt infused with cracked black pepper and beer, and the Queso mixed with cilantro, roasted peppers, and sweet onions. Lamb, sausage, and Asian-style teriyaki are ready for dipping, and the garlicky Swiss cheese fondue is served with cushy cubes of bread and fried potatoes. On the sweet side, there's a heavenly dark chocolate fondue and the ooey-gooey Marshmallow Dream fondue served with crumbled butter cookies.

THE GREATEST: California Wine List

Sonoma $$$
206 Worcester Rd., Princeton, MA, (978) 464-5775
www.sonoma-princeton.com
This treasure is hidden away in the hills of Princeton. But Sonoma is worth seeking out for both its unforgettable fare and an amazing California wine list. Kitchen highlights include creamy pumpkin soup served in a hollow pumpkin, and their "pastrami on rye": a pepper-crusted duckling served with lavender-honey mustard. Phantom also loves the mushroom-dusted rib chop. To top off the meal, the decadent dessert tray rolls up with tasty treats like pumpkin cheesecake and chocolate custard cake with chocolate shavings.

THE GREATEST: Mac and Cheese

Silvertone $$
69 Bromfield St., Boston, MA, (617) 338-7887
Silvertone attracts a twenty-something cocktail crowd to its below-ground retro digs. The unbelievably affordable menu includes homey comfort foods like creamy cheddar mac and cheese encrusted with golden bread crumbs, served in an oversized soufflé dish with a side of greens. Phantom adores their roasted pepper quesadillas and diner-style, gravy-slathered meatloaf on mashed potatoes. Their wine list is the best value around, since they refuse to mark a bottle up more than $10 from retail. Silvertone's stylish old-school decorations include vintage radios, weathered photos, and high-backed booths.

Cookies
GREAT ATE

THE GREATEST: Chocolate Chip Cookies

The Boston Chipyard $$$
257 Faneuil Hall Marketplace, Boston, MA, (617) 742-9537
www.chipyard.com

Every single cookie at the Chipyard is made with chocolate chips, but there's still plenty of variety. Beyond the best-selling Traditional Chocolate Chip, these morsels go into Oatmeal Raisin Chocolate Chip and Peanut Butter Chocolate Chip cookies. White Chocolate Chip is a spin on the original, and Mint Chocolate Chip flies off the shelf like hotcakes. Chunkier varieties include macadamia nuts and walnuts. Chipyard cookies are pretty petit, so they're perfect for snacking or sharing.

THE GREATEST: Oversized Cookies

Dunkin' Donuts $
5,000 locations worldwide
www.dunkindonuts.com

Everyone knows Dunkin' Donuts as a go-to spot for quick, consistent coffee and chocolate-glazed donuts. But their test kitchen has been baking up a storm, adding jumbo cookies to their sugary arsenal. At three times the size of the average snack, they're simply irresistible. Indulgent flavors include oatmeal raisin loaded with cinnamon, gooey chocolate chip, and peanut butter cup made with huge hunks of candy. Check out their other innovations like the Supreme Omelet on a croissant.

THE GREATEST: Cookie Tin

A Dozen Eggs $$
(617) 650-0048
www.adozeneggs.com

Specializing in iced sugar cookies, A Dozen Eggs turns famous Boston landmarks into edible art. Their signature Beantown Cookie Tin is packed with sweet treats that look like the Citgo sign, the T, floating swan boats, and even a Red Sox jersey. They bake specialty cookies for every season, including snowflakes in winter, flowers for spring, and leaves in the fall. The best way to get a bite of Beantown is to order online a tin of these crunchy, buttery cookies.

THE GREATEST: **Skillet Cookie**

Bugaboo Creek Steak House $$
12 Massachusetts locations
www.bugaboocreeksteakhouse.com

Bugaboo Creek is a fun chain set up like a mountain lodge. Phantom likes to hike over for the seven-inch Big Foot Chocolate Cookie. Presented in an iron skillet, this gooey chocolate chip cookie is baked on a graham cracker crust and topped with vanilla ice cream. It's warm, soft, and absolutely irresistible. But first, work up an appetite with some blackened shrimp and a Moosebreath Burger. The rustic lodge décor is one-of-a-kind, featuring fishing gear, a stone fireplace, and Moxie, the talking moose.

THE GREATEST: **Half-Moon**

Lyndell's Bakery $
720 Broadway, Somerville, MA, (617) 625-1793

Dating back to 1887, Lyndell's Bakery is still worth its weight in cake flour. Italian pastries pack the cases, but don't dare leave without a half-moon in hand. This black-and-white cookie is for icing lovers only, with a fluffy cake supporting twice as much vanilla-on-chocolate frosting. Lyndell's cookie selection also includes molasses, praline, and butter-crunch varieties. They do honey-dipped donuts, incredible cinnamon buns, frosted cupcakes, and flaky elephant ears. Rainbow birthday cakes line the front window, and servers use a special machine to wrap the cookie boxes with string.

THE GREATEST: **"Oreos"**

Flour Bakery $
1595 Washington St., Boston, MA, (617) 267-4300
www.flourbakery.com

The gourmet "Oreos" at Flour Bakery blow away the store-bought brand. Their rich, chocolaty rendition sandwiches deep, dark, snappy cookies around a creamy filling. The flavor changes occasionally to peanut butter or fresh mint. Flour makes a mean chocolate chip cookie with high-end Scharffen Berger chips, and the meringue clouds are light as can be. Breads, pizza, and quiche fill out the tempting display, plus pastries like chocolate brioche, sticky buns, and sour cream coffee cake. At lunch you'll find sandwiches such as the BLT with applewood-smoked bacon.

THE GREATEST: Iced Sugar Cookies

Hi-Rise Bread Company $

208 Concord Ave., Cambridge, MA, (617) 876-8766

Hi-Rise crafts the most incredible iced sugar cookies around. Each colorful piece is decorated with cute animals like sheep and bunnies. Adults adore their pretty, puffy almond macaroons; and the chocolate chunk cookies are big enough to make a meal. Hi-Rise also makes one of the wispiest lemon meringue pies Phantom has ever tasted, as well as made-to-order sandwiches like the Nat Queen Cool with pulled pork, avocado, and cilantro. Customers can sink into an antique booth and watch the bakers kneading loaves of walnut, olive, and cheddar-pepper bread. There's a smaller Hi-Rise in Harvard Square.

THE GREATEST: Dark Chocolate Cookie

Rosie's Bakery $

6 Massachusetts locations

www.rosiesbakery.com

Rosie's Bakery whips up amazing pastries, coffee with whipped cream, and beautiful tarts. But it's their Soho Glob that has Phantom coming back again and again. Like a decadent dark chocolate brownie in cookie form, this chewy treat is absolutely packed with pecans, walnuts, and chocolate chips. Speaking of brownies, the Chocolate Orgasm is scandalously rich and frosted with fudge. Cinnamon rolls, buttercream iced cakes, and savory stuffed croissants round out the offerings. Locations include Cambridge, Chestnut Hill, Lexington, South Station, Porter Square, and Wellesley.

Dessert
GREAT ATE

THE GREATEST: **Dessert Course**

Finale $$
1 Columbus Ave., Boston, MA, (617) 423-3184
www.finaledesserts.com

Defying the mantra of mothers everywhere, Finale insists that dessert comes first. This elegant "desserterie" serves light meals and hot toddies, but it's the gorgeous cookies, cakes, and chocolates that are the main course for most diners. They're open late for the post-theater crowd, perfecting signature dishes like molten chocolate cake and crème brûlée smothered in six kinds of fresh fruit. Phantom favors the bittersweet Manjari mousse and the Boston cream pie served with mini whoopie pies. Additional locations include Harvard Square and Coolidge Corner.

THE GREATEST: **Cheesecake**

Cheesecake Factory $$
115 Huntington Ave., S. 181, Boston, MA, (617) 399-7777
www.thecheesecakefactory.com

The Cheesecake Factory boasts the biggest menu Phantom has ever seen; the dessert section alone lists 30 tantalizing cheesecake flavors. There's the creamy original wedged into a buttery graham cracker crust, with fresh strawberries as a quick upgrade. The rest of the menu gets downright creative, with options like chocolate raspberry truffle, chocolate chip cookie dough, Key lime, and white chocolate. There's Godiva chocolate cheesecake, tiramisu cheesecake, and even carrot cake and cheesecake mixed together in one decadent dessert. Phantom also loves the Cheesecake Factory for oversized entrées and fun finger foods like bite-sized burgers and crispy macaroni and cheese balls.

THE GREATEST: **Pie**

Petsi Pies $
285 Beacon St., Somerville, MA, (617) 661-PIES
www.petsipies.com

Petsi Pies is a small storefront turning out perfect pies. Their secret lies in the rich, flaky crust baked to a golden hue. The apple pie is nothing short of awesome, but there's also pecan pie and whoopie pie. The house specialties are all

Southern, including sweet potato pie spiced with ginger and brown sugar. Phantom loves the peach blueberry pie bursting with ripe fruit and the potato mushroom tart layered with roasted red bliss potatoes, fresh rosemary, and Gruyère cheese. There's a second location in Cambridge on Putnam Avenue.

THE GREATEST: Baked Alaska

Oleana
134 Hampshire St., Cambridge, MA, (617) 661-0505
www.oleanarestaurant.com
Oleana one-ups desserts on the fine dining circuit with their legendary baked Alaska. The huge hot-cold creation is unforgettable, served as a wispy mass of meringue around homemade coconut ice cream, all sitting on a chewy coconut crust surrounded by passion fruit caramel. There's also a frozen chocolate mint soufflé and sweet nougat glace with peach confit. Besides dessert, the Arabic-influenced menu infuses exotic spices into dishes like Turkish lamb steak with fava bean moussaka. Plus, you can order pre-appetizers like deviled eggs with tuna and black olives. Oleana has an inviting bar and opens its garden patio in warmer weather.

THE GREATEST: Nor'easter

Joe Fish
1120 Osgood St. (Rt. 125), North Andover, MA, (978) 685-3663
www.joefish.net
Joe Fish storms into the Dessert Great Ate with the Nor'easter ice cream sundae that comes to the table in a cloud of "fog" created by ice. Under the haze lies a delicious tornado of brownies, chocolate chip cookies, and vanilla and chocolate ice cream. It's absolutely smothered in whipped cream, hot fudge, fruit, and gooey caramel. Before the grand finale, you can work up an appetite with succulent seafood. Highlights include shrimp cocktail, flash-fried yellowfin tuna, and fried oysters with French fries. There's even a lobster stuffed with more lobster. Joe Fish has a sister restaurant next door called The Loft Steak and Chop House, and it offers the same Nor'easter sundae plus lobster mac and cheese.

THE GREATEST: Dessert Bar

Petit Robert Bistro $$
468 Commonwealth Ave., Boston, MA, (617) 375-0699
www.petitrobertbistro.com
Petit Robert Bistro is so dedicated to sweets, they've built a dessert bar where you can watch the pastry chef put on a sugary show. Their signature gâteau includes a

rich cut of chocolate ganache cake finished with shaved white chocolate and topped by an edible Eiffel Tower made out of chocolate. There's also a warm tarte Tatin crafted with candied apples as big as doorknobs, finished with creamy crème fraîche. Petit Robert serves affordable bistro fare like French onion soup and skirt steak smothered in bordelaise. It's a great place to eat before heading to see the Red Sox, and there's a second location on Columbus Avenue in the South End.

THE GREATEST: Whoopie Pie

Wicked Whoopies $

5 Mechanic St., Gardiner, ME, (877) 447-2629
www.wickedwhoopies.com

Wicked Whoopies is *the* authority on making whoopie. Whoopie pies, that is! Just when you thought the original recipe of whipped cream between devil's food cake couldn't get any better, Isamax Snacks has redefined it with 20 flavors and variations. Phantom's favorites include strawberry, chocolate chip, and raspberry and cream. There's also a whopping five-pound Wicked Whoopie and a chocolate-dipped Whoop-de-Doo that's like a gourmet Ring Ding. Customers can buy Wicked Whoopies online or at the tiny, bright retail shop in Gardiner, Maine.

THE GREATEST: Ice Cream Desserts

Trani $

111 Salem St., Boston, MA, (617) 624-0222
www.tranibrand.com

Trani brings a dessert list to the North End like the world has never seen. Every cannoli, donut, and brownie is injected with cool, creamy ice cream. After the customer picks from a dozen different pastries, it's placed on a custom-built machine and injected with a creamy core. Thicker than traditional soft serve, this delicious filling is made from a secret recipe that's silky smooth. If cramming a cupcake with ice cream isn't indulgent enough, the whole thing can be coated in warm chocolate, which hardens for a crispy, crunchy, over-the-top treat.

Diners
GREAT ATE

THE GREATEST: **Milkshake**

'50s Diner $
5 Commercial Cir., Dedham, MA, (781) 326-1955

The '50s Diner is dedicated to the decade of doo-wop and bobby socks. They have posters of Marilyn Monroe and Elvis on the walls, as well as a Coca-Cola cooler. The cramped kitchen cranks out big breakfasts like strawberry-smothered Belgian waffles and Texas French toast finished with bananas and powdered sugar. The Everything Omelet spills over with broccoli, spinach, tomato, onion, pepper, mushroom, bacon, sausage, ham, and cheese. Phantom loves their bacon cheeseburger, and the rich and creamy milkshakes are so impossibly thick, you could bust a lung trying to suck one up the straw.

THE GREATEST: **Retro Diner**

MaryAnn's Diner $
29 E. Broadway, Derry, NH, (603) 434-5785,
www.maryannsdiner.com

MaryAnn's Diner is extraordinarily retro, decked out in glowing neon signs, an old-fashioned jukebox, and an antique Texaco gas pump. The waitresses dress in poodle skirts and ponytails, and pictures of American icons from the '50s and '60s cover the walls with characters like Elvis, James Dean, and Marilyn Monroe. The first-rate diner food comes in portions that test even Phantom's legendary appetite. The home fries are crisp and crusty; the savory sausage and gravy comes on a toasted biscuit; and the waffles are piled high with strawberries, blueberries, and vanilla ice cream.

THE GREATEST: **Late-Night Diner**

Kenmore Diner $
250 Franklin St., Worcester, MA, (508) 792-5125

When the late-night munchies hit, the Kenmore Diner steps up to the blue plate by opening its doors from 11 p.m. until the following afternoon, every day except Monday and Sunday. The location is slightly spooky, hidden under exit 14 of Route 290, but it's the perfect greasy reward to a night on the town. A massive renovation due to a fire has turned the Kenmore into a sparklingly clean and modern restaurant featuring a checkerboard floor. Shiny red booths match the counter stools, which line up across from the sizzling open grill. Breakfast is served all night long, featuring classic eggs, pancakes, burgers, cheesecake, and strong coffee.

THE GREATEST: Baked Ham

Dream Diner $
384 Middlesex Rd., Tyngsboro, MA, (978) 649-7097
www.dreamdiner.com
If there were a spirit award for diner atmosphere, Dream Diner would win the blue plate ribbon. Past the antique convertibles out front, the vintage Coca-Cola motif takes over, bolstered by red vinyl booths and counter stools. Breakfast is served all day, with sweet potato pancakes and three dozen omelets named after original diner car companies. Top-notch lunch plates include the spinach and feta Greek burger, and nothing says nostalgia better than their chocolaty, creamy whoopie pies. Before exploring awesome dishes like the crock of chicken pot pie sealed in puff pastry, newbies should initiate themselves with the incredible baked ham, carved off the bone in thick, juicy slices.

THE GREATEST: Original Architecture

Casey's Diner $
36 South Ave., Natick, MA, (508) 655-3761
Slide open the door to Casey's Diner, and find yourself back at the turn of the century. Everything, including the floor and (arguably) the prices, is from the original diner. Casey's is housed in a 1922 Worcester diner car, which is like a tiny torpedo of a lunch cart that barely squeezes 10 swivel stools along the counter. The all-oak interior is well worn, the take-out window gets a good workout, and the gas stove still sports porcelain handles. Serving up chopped ham sandwiches and apple pie, the short-order cooks are best known for the All-Around Hot Dog, which is absolutely smothered in relish, onion, and mustard.

THE GREATEST: Atypical Diner Menu

Rosebud Diner $
381 Summer St., Somerville, MA, (617) 666-6015
www.rosebuddiner.com
The Rosebud Diner is a genuine throwback to the '50s, with a tasty atypical menu. Their wide-ranging beverage repertoire includes wine, microbrews on tap, and stiff Bloody Marys. The kitchen turns out comfort food with Phantom favorites like the Cajun char-burger with jalapeño cheese, Flamin' Wings, nachos, and mushrooms

doused in spicy sauce and blue cheese. The atmosphere in the 1941 Worcester dining car is quite authentic, complete with sassy, seasoned waitresses and vintage blue tiling.

THE GREATEST: **Reuben Sandwich**

Sunny Day Diner $
Rte. 3, Lincoln, NH, (603) 745-4833

Tucked away in the White Mountains, Sunny Day Diner is the ultimate blue plate experience. It's a cheery roadside destination with chrome-lined atmosphere and Phantom's favorite Reuben sandwich. Two hefty layers of warm corned beef are topped with juicy beer-baked sauerkraut, a thick slab of Swiss cheese, and tangy dressing on grilled marbled rye. The in-house baker turns out breads, berry-studded muffins, cakes, crumb-topped pies, and old-fashioned ice cream. Fresh-squeezed orange juice and cobb-smoked bacon are perfect with any plate.

THE GREATEST: **Diner Dinner**

Jigger's Diner $
145 Main St., East Greenwich, RI, (401) 884-5388

From the outside, Jigger's Diner looks like a typical stainless steel snack spot. But every Friday and Saturday night, they take a break from bacon and eggs and go gourmet. This Worcester dining car transforms into a fine dining destination with low lights, candles, and wine glasses. The BYOB dinner menu changes weekly, but it always includes salad and soups like shrimp and crab bisque. Entrées might be pork loin stuffed with roasted red peppers, prosciutto, and Gorgonzola, or pancetta-wrapped chicken breast over tomato basil pappardelle. Kiddies can come for dinner, too, and order grilled cheese or hot dogs.

Dining Bargains
GREAT ATE

THE GREATEST: Giant Subs

Dino's $
141 Salem St., Boston, MA, (617) 227-1991
www.dinosboston.com

Dino's is *the* speedy spot for no-frills feasts in the North End. Belly-busting 16-inch subs come in hot and cold variations. The Sicilian steak sub is topped with mushrooms and tomatoes, and the chicken Parm wears a gooey blend of sauce and melted cheese. The Italian sub is a packed classic of provolone, salami, mortadella, capicola ham, oil, vinegar, and hot peppers. Phantom strongly advises *not* asking for a half-sandwich, and to *definitely* have your cash ready and in hand. You gotta play by the house rules for food this abundant and cheap.

THE GREATEST: Steak Tips

New Bridge Café $
650 Washington Ave., Chelsea, MA, (617) 884-0134

New Bridge Café is the wallet-friendly cure for a steak craving. Their steak tips are the best in New England. Seventy-five percent of their business comes from juicy, sought-after tips, which also include lamb tips, pork tips, and turkey tips. There's a fantastic rack of baby back ribs. Whether you settle into a vinyl booth or opt for a seat at the bar, nothing on the TV will distract your attention from the sweet sauce covering these succulent cubes of meat. No wonder they won't spill the secret ingredients in the marinade.

THE GREATEST: Price Buster Menu

Halfway Café $$
174 Washington St., Dedham, MA, (781) 326-3336
www.thehalfwaycafe.com

The Halfway Café lives up to its "good food cheap" slogan with nearly every menu item ringing up at less than $12. They even sweeten the pot with a daily Price Buster meal for $7.99. The weekly schedule rotates through featured entrées like steak tips, stuffed shells, country fried chicken, pot roast, and fried clam strips. Guilty pleasures fill the rest of menu, with Phantom favorites like the Smokehouse Burger with BBQ sauce, "buzz"-sauce pork tips, meatball pizzas, and steamers.

The café has a comfortable feel with wooden tables and booths, a stocked bar, and scores of framed sports photos on the walls. Locations include Dedham, Marlboro, Watertown, and Canton.

THE GREATEST: $2 Bar Menu

Daisy Buchanan's $
240 Newbury St., Boston, MA, (617) 247-8516
Trendy Newbury Street seems like the last place to find a Boston bargain, but that's exactly what you'll discover at Daisy Buchanan's. This dirt-cheap dive gets even less expensive with a $2 bar menu Sunday through Thursday from 3 to 7 p.m. Offerings include cheddar bacon burgers, grilled cheese, all-beef hot dogs, bruschetta and minestrone soup. For a couple bucks more, you can score seafood like crab cakes and steamers. There's never a cover, and though it's a big draw for college kids, the place is famous for celebrity sightings. Red Sox players come by late at night, and the beautiful waitresses from Ciao Bella descend the stairs when they finish their shift.

THE GREATEST: 99-Cent Pizza

Emma's Pub & Pizza $
1420 Pleasant St., Bridgewater, MA, (508) 697-8815
www.emmaspubandpizza.com
Serving up meal deals every day of the week, Emma's Pub & Pizza is unbeatable for its 99-cent cheese pizzas on Sundays (1 to 4 p.m.) and Wednesdays (8:30 to 10:30 p.m.). The place gets mobbed with kids on Monday and Wednesday nights (6 to 8 p.m.) when there is a magician in the house. Tuesday is the all-you-can-eat fajita frenzy, and Thursdays feature half-price appetizers from 8 to 11 p.m. Emma's regular menu includes 20-ounce steak tips and the half-pound Titanic Lobster Roll.

THE GREATEST: Bar Bites

Morton's $
One Exeter Plaza, 699 Boylston at Exeter, Boston, MA, (617) 266-5858
www.mortons.com
Morton's is a high-end steak house, but their BAR 12*21 offers one of the best bargains in Greater Boston. Specially priced "Bar Bites" cost as little as $1.50 and no more than $4 per plate from 5 to 6:30 p.m. and again from 9:30 to 11 p.m., Monday through Friday. Offerings include oysters on the half shell, filet mignon sandwiches, Prime cheeseburger sliders, "colossal" shrimp, and creamy crab dip. If continuing into the dining room, expect waiters to wheel a physical menu right to the table, displaying Maine lobster and juicy Prime aged steaks.

THE GREATEST: Bargain Lunch

Bukowski Tavern $
50 Dalton St., Boston, MA, (617) 437-9999
Bukowski Tavern is home of the Steal of a Meal Lunch Deal. Burgers are usually $9, but from noon to 8 p.m. on weekdays, they're just $1.69 each. Hot dogs are just as economical, and it's $1.10 for extra toppings like cheese. You can wash it all down with a choice of 100 different bottled beers. Their uncommonly good pub grub includes White Trash Cheese Dip, and the corkscrew mac and cheese comes with broccoli and chorizo. The sweet potato fries pair with Dijon horseradish sauce, and oddities like the peanut butter burger are surprisingly tasty. There's a second, more stylish location in Inman Square, Cambridge.

THE GREATEST: Cheap Burritos

Anna's Taqueria $
1412 Beacon St., Brookline, MA, (617) 739-7300
www.annastaqueria.com
Anna's Taqueria in Brookline, Cambridge, and Somerville serves the best burritos for next to nothing. The massive tortilla wraps are made-to-order with a choice of pulled chicken, grilled steak, veggies, or pork carnitas. As soon as the tortilla comes out of the steamer, customers rattle off what they want: beans, rice, salsa, lettuce, guacamole, or hot sauce. The whole process takes 30 seconds, and it's handed off on a real plate with real silverware. Though the food is cheap, you can still enjoy homey touches like wooden chairs and tables and even chandeliers.

Eight Top Tables
GREAT ATE

THE GREATEST: **Balcony Table**

Tresca $$$
233 Hanover St., Boston, MA, (617) 742-8240
www.trescanorthend.com
Tresca brings the latest taste of regional Italian cuisine to the North End, and it's
best enjoyed at their only balcony table. Hanging over Hanover Street, the cozy
open-air table for two barely has enough space for a server to take the order. It of-
fers an amazing bird's-eye view of the city and the hustle and bustle below.
Tresca's menu includes pappardelle pasta with wild mushrooms and lobster risotto
topped with an entire lobster tail. It's one of the only eateries where you can order
a steak as an appetizer; the four-ounce bone-in Filetto Piccolo comes with fire-
roasted peppers and Parmigiano-Reggiano.

THE GREATEST: **Exclusive Dining**

Newburyport Lighthouse $$$
61 ½ Water St., Newburyport, MA, (800) 727-BEAM
www.lighthousepreservation.org
For the ultimate romantic dinner, the Newburyport Lighthouse provides a unique
private dining experience for two. Guests ascend 55 steps and settle in for a lunch
or dinner of panoramic scenery and a spectacular multicourse meal. The town's top
restaurants offer their cooking, including the Black Cow and Blue Water Cafe.
Reservations are required months in advance for the season (April to December).
It's a worthy splurge of $300 to reserve the space, which is mostly tax-deductible
and includes gratuity and a membership to the Lighthouse Preservation Society.
Food and drink are priced per restaurant, and service extends for six scenic hours.

THE GREATEST: **Lobster Picnic**

Chauncey Creek Lobster Pier $$
16 Chauncey Creek Rd., Kittery Point, ME, (207) 439-1030
www.chaunceycreek.com
Chauncey Creek Lobster Pier is a rare treasure that combines outdoor dining with
clambake cuisine. Crayola-colored picnic tables line the deck, and Phantom's fa-
vorite seats are along the edge, jutting out over the spectacular Maine waters.

Chauncey Creek is worth the trek for the fresh-air ambiance alone, but the awesome food rounds out the experience. Head to the seafood shack and choose from a New England menu of boiled lobster, fresh crab rolls, steamed mussels in garlic and wine, chowder, and peel-and-eat shrimp. Customers can supplement the meal by bringing extra sides, wine, or beer.

THE GREATEST: Newbury Street Scene

Ciao Bella $$$
240A Newbury St., Boston, MA, (617) 536-2626
www.ciaobella.com

Ciao Bella is high profile real estate on Newbury Street, and it's *the* place to see and be seen in Boston. Every table offers romantic atmosphere, but Table 3 is the most sought-after seat in the house. Flush against a glass-encased extension over the sidewalk, it's like a box seat at the theater. It's not surprising, then, that celebrities such as David Letterman have insisted on sitting there. When it comes to cooking, there are two things to remember: chops and more chops. Ciao Bella's kitchen has built its reputation on the 18-ounce "Jurassic" veal chop, and their special thick-cut swordfish chop is roasted and plated with tomatoes, basil, and black olives.

THE GREATEST: Spice Bar

Masala Art $$$
990 Great Plain Ave., Needham, MA, (781) 449-4050
www.masala-art.com

Masala Art claims to have the nation's only spice bar, where customers participate in an interactive Indian meal. The chef explains the art of blending spices over a multi-course feast. It's all cooked right before your eyes on an authentic Indian pan that looks like a flattened wok. The dining room is trendy and stylish, and customers can order kebabs or barbecued lamb chops that are incredibly tender thanks to three days spent marinating in yogurt. The coconut tamarind chicken comes in a creamy curry, and every entrée pairs well with puffy naan bread. If you can't get a stool at the spice bar, the blue-lit cocktail bar is a fun place to spend the night, too.

THE GREATEST: Rooftop Dining

Ristorante Fiore $$
250 Hanover St., Boston, MA, (617) 371-1176
www.ristorantefiore.com

Dining in the North End is always special; dining on a North End rooftop is paradise. Fiore is one of the biggest restaurants in Boston's Little Italy, and it's one of the only restaurants in the city with rooftop dining. Their light, airy pizzas are delicious topped with shrimp and pesto or mozzarella and thin-sliced prosciutto. The strength of the menu is seafood, like the swordfish with garlic and white wine or the home-made pasta with lobster and shrimp in vodka sauce.

THE GREATEST: Olive Oil Table

Miel $$
InterContinental Boston, 510 Atlantic Ave., Boston, MA, (617) 747-1000
www.intercontinentalboston.com

Late-night restaurants in Boston are about as common as Yankee fans, so Phantom is ecstatic that Miel keeps its doors open around the clock. This brasserie-style eatery features light Provençal foods of southern France. Highlights include chick-pea crepes, bouillabaisse seafood stew, and seared scallops with honey vinaigrette. Miel's "olive oil museum" is a private glass-enclosed dining room for 12 people. It features a chef's table carved from a 1,000-year-old olive tree and an olive oil chan-delier shaped like a honeycomb. There's also an extensive collection of imported oils from seven countries displayed in an 18-foot tower. (Kind of like a wine cellar, but greasier.)

THE GREATEST: People-Watching

Plaza III $$$
Faneuil Hall Marketplace, Boston, MA, (617) 720-5570
www.plazaiiisteakhouse.com

Plaza III offers tasty Prime beef from Kansas City, but the real reason to eat here is the corner seat outside. As the crossroads of the North End, the Financial District, and Government Center, this roped-off area is *the* Faneuil Hall hotspot for people-watching. At Plaza III, the "menu" is wheeled to the table so customers can choose from a visual presentation of corn-fed beef, thick chops, and seafood. The meaty steak soup is their signature starter, and steaks are aged in a temperature-controlled beef locker.

Ethnic
GREAT ATE

THE GREATEST: Polish Restaurant

Café Polonia   **$$**
611 Dorchester St., South Boston, MA, (617) 269-0110
www.cafepolonia.com

As Boston's only Polish restaurant, Café Polonia provides relief from pretentious urban dining. The stone-walled space is barely big enough for six sturdy pine tables, and they keep the polka music pumping. The menu stars robust traditional dishes of potatoes, cabbage, and meat, as well as Eastern European specialties and a great selection of Polish beer. Every table starts with sliced bread and a tasty spread of bacon-flecked lard. Entrées like potato pancakes and goulash are rib-sticking delicious. Phantom also recommends the potato pierogi dumplings and kielbasa sausage. Their sister store across the street sells Polish groceries and newspapers.

THE GREATEST: Afghani Cuisine

The Helmand   **$$**
143 First St., Cambridge, MA, (617) 492-4646
www.helmand.restaurantcambridge.com

Cambridge may be New England's best city for ethnic cuisine. Supporting this case is the Helmand, in the shadow of the CambridgeSide Galleria. Decorated with country cupboards and a working fireplace, it has a colorful, homey atmosphere that feels like a festive dinner party. They bake flatbread right in the dining room in a wood-fired oven and serve it with herb sauces and yogurt for dipping. Vegetarians love the eggplant concoctions and pan-fried pumpkin, carnivores steer toward the incredible lamb dishes, and everyone enjoys the aromatic baked rice infused with cardamom, cinnamon, nutmeg, cumin, and black pepper.

THE GREATEST: Cuban-French Fusion

Chez Henri   **$$$**
One Shepard St., Cambridge, MA, (617) 354-8980
www.chezhenri.com

Chez Henri is a Cuban-French bistro with one-of-a-kind fusion cuisine. It's the best of both worlds, a place where you can sip fresh mint mojitos while digging into steak frites slathered in garlicky chimichurri sauce. The island influence brings chile-glazed tuna and coconut lime ceviche to the plate. But you can also score smoked pork ribs in a guava BBQ sauce. The bistro setting is sexy with low lighting and bright still lifes painted by the chef's wife. The more casual bar side is famous for its pressed Cubano sandwich stuffed with slow-roasted pork. And they now offer a bocadillo menu of $10 small bites.

THE GREATEST: Tamales, Tostadas, and Tacos

Taqueria Cancun $$
192 Sumner St., Boston, MA, (617) 567-4449

You won't need much cash at this East Boston taqueria, where the tamales, tostadas, and tacos are irresistible. The menu is Mexican meets Salvadoran, which means lots of tortillas, rice, and beans. Phantom especially loves their enchiladas piled with spicy pork, guacamole, pico de gallo, and sour cream. The pupusas, or ground-corn cakes, are stuffed with meat and beans, and the Montanero plate is a Phantom-sized feast of flank steak, fried egg over rice, and glistening pork rinds. Definitely save room for desserts like sweet plantain empanadas.

THE GREATEST: Thai Food

Brown Sugar Cafe $
1033 Commonwealth Ave., Boston, MA, (617) 787-4242
www.brownsugarcafe.com

Brown Sugar Cafe is a sweet name for a restaurant that serves hot Thai food. It's Phantom's top choice for eating on the cheap without compromising on flavor. The never-ending menu rivals the Cheesecake Factory's in length, with an incredible range of rice dishes, noodles, and hot pots. The best appetizers are fresh rolls wound with basil and shrimp and curry potato karee puff pastries. Brown Sugar pulls out all the stops on presentation for dishes like the shrimp curry Virgin Island served in a coconut shell. Others arrive spilling out of pineapple shells, and the restaurant displays fish tanks and Thai tapestries, making for a colorful atmosphere.

THE GREATEST: Cape Verdean Cuisine

Restaurante Cesaria $$
266 Bowdoin St., Dorchester, MA, (617) 282-1998
www.restaurantecesaria.com

Run by a staff that's brimming with ethnic pride, Cesaria salutes its colorful Cape Verdean roots with Portuguese-African fusion. Plates range from the familiar to the exotic, and there's plenty of sauced seafood, rice, and beans. Phantom begins with garlic-infused linguica sausage and sweet fried yucca paired with honey mustard for dipping. The house specialty, katchupada, is a stick-to-your-ribs porridge of hominy, fatty pork, rock beans, and kale. A baby grand piano adds to the party atmosphere in the spacious dining room.

THE GREATEST: Mediterranean Meal

Sabur $$

212 Holland St., Somerville, MA, (617) 776-7890

www.saburrestaurant.com

With handcrafted copper tables and the scent of 100-year-old recipes cooking away, Sabur transports you straight to southeastern Europe. It's a two-room space where sheer curtains and woven pillows make you feel like you're miles away from Teal Square. Many of the recipes on the exotic menu originate near Bosnia, where the owner was born. Flavorful Mediterranean dishes include Italian seafood stew packed with cod, clams, mussels, and shrimp. The house specialty is an unforgettable feast of lamb and vegetables, slow-roasted in an open hearth right in the dining room.

THE GREATEST: Turkish Takeout

Sultan's Kitchen $

116 State St., Boston, MA, (617) 570-9009

www.sultans-kitchen.com

Sultan's Kitchen is Boston's top Turkish restaurant and a healthy alternative to standard fast food. Financial District workers flock here for flavorful, affordable dishes that range from subtle to spicy. The tiny, bright space gets absolutely jammed at lunch, as customers stream past the open kitchen lined with gorgeous platters of baba ghanoush eggplant spread, stuffed grape leaves, and pita sandwiches overflowing with lamb shish kebabs. Cucumber tomato salad and light rice pilaf come with the grilled meat platters, and the spicy Peynirli flatbread looks like a personal pizza topped with green peppers, olives, and feta. The kitchen closes at 4 p.m. on Saturday and 8:30 p.m. from Monday to Friday.

THE GREATEST: French Fries

McDonald's   **$**
30,000 locations
www.mcdonalds.com

McDonald's sublimely salty, crunchy shoestring fries are the king of the category. These days, new Golden Arches are upgraded with flat-screen TVs, chandeliers, and Wi-Fi access. Despite all the imitations out there, the Quarter Pounder remains a fast food classic. The Chicken McNuggets are now all white meat, and they're pretty darn tasty. Phantom hates to admit it, but the addition of salads and fruit has helped revive this American icon. Kids Meals now come with apple dippers and milk or juice.

THE GREATEST: Fast Food Burger

Wendy's   **$**
6,000 locations
www.wendys.com

Wendy's remains the classiest of the Big Three (topping McDonald's and Burger King). Since founder Dave Thomas went to that great drive-thru in the sky, the chain hasn't missed a beat. The trademark square burgers are so delicious that Phantom once ate what he calls "the cycle": a single, double, triple, and Big Bacon Classic in one sitting. The salads are a more interactive experience than Phantom would like (at last count there were three separate packets to open and add to the bowl), but they're fresh and filling. The baked potato is a great option for a fast food place, and Phantom is also a Phan of the cheddar-topped chili and the extra-thick Frosty.

THE GREATEST: Quick, Classy Sandwiches

Cosi   **$**
80 locations
www.xandocosi.com

Cosi is an East Coast legend that originated in Paris. The trendy atmosphere includes wooden tables and a sandwich bar, where selections are made to order. But their competitive advantage lies in crusty flatbread baked in hearth-fired ovens, right in the middle of the restaurant. Customers can snack on samples while they wait, and then choose from splendid sandwich fillers like spinach artichoke spread, caramelized onions, and tandoori grilled chicken. The State Street Cosi gets a lot of Financial District business, and anyone with Wi-Fi capabilities can "surf and sip" at the Milk Street and Federal Street locations.

THE GREATEST: Mexican Munchies

Baja Fresh $
300 locations
www.bajafresh.com
A mere baby compared to the fast food behemoths, Baja Fresh may expand faster than Phantom's purple waistline. The design is sleek with black-and-white checkered floors and raised tables. Defying fast food tradition, Baja sports an open kitchen with no shortcuts like can openers or microwaves. This Tex-Mex grill bangs out everything on site as ordered, with only a 10-minute wait. Phantom enjoys the crunchy toasted nachos stacked generously with chunky salsa, melted jack, cheddar cheese, and guacamole. If you like a little spice, there's a self-service salsa bar.

THE GREATEST: Toasted Sandwiches

Quiznos Sub $
4,000 locations
www.quiznos.com
Quiznos's toasted bread strategy has turned up the heat on national competitors like Panera Bread and D'Angelo. The added crunch makes a big difference, and their ingredients are better than the average chain. Phantom enjoys the mesquite chicken with ranch dressing and the prime rib sub with peppercorn sauce and sautéed onions. They even have a Bistro Beef on cheddar onion ciabatta bread, and the turkey sub teams with bacon and avocado.

THE GREATEST: Pizza Delivery

Papa John's $
3,000 locations
www.papajohns.com
What really sets Papa John's apart is the garlic butter they serve on the side. It's so potent and delicious that Phantom would eat his shoe if it were slathered in the stuff. A lot of fast food places add so many items that the counter menu looks like a Las Vegas sports book. To its credit, Papa John's has stayed focused on its streamlined pizza selection, along with eight dipping sauces. Papa John's locations aren't real pretty, so Phantom recommends takeout or delivery. It couldn't be easier thanks to online ordering.

THE GREATEST: **Rapid Roast Beef**

Arby's $
3,500 locations
www.arbys.com

Kelly's Roast Beef owns the local market for roast beef, but Arby's does this sand-wich delicacy best on a national level. It's what Phantom would call a "highway chain," meaning he only visits one when he's 1) ravenously hungry and 2) doesn't want to stray off the driving route. The Beef 'n Cheddar sandwich is the star offer-ing, featuring lean roast beef, cheddar cheese sauce, and a special dressing served on a grilled onion bun. The Big Montana is a half-pound mountain of roast beef jacked up on a toasted sesame seed bun.

THE GREATEST: **Fried Chicken**

Popeye's Chicken & Biscuits $
1,800 locations
www.popeyes.com

Phantom is a huge KFC fan, and he's gone on record saying they still make the sin-gle best coleslaw into which he's ever dug a spork. However, Popeye's still out-muscles the Colonel. Fried chicken is the foundation of the New Orleans–inspired menu, and most sides, like the fries, are Cajun spiced. The fried chicken is crispy and crunchy on the outside, but moist and juicy inside. It comes in mild or spicy hot, and you can also enjoy the moist meat on a sandwich with mayo or mixed into jambalaya. Instead of standard fried sides, get crazy and try the Cajun rice and some flaky buttermilk biscuits. Bay State locations include the Westgate Mall in Brockton and a new Fenway store on Beacon Street.

Local Fast Food
GREAT ATE

THE GREATEST: Burritos and Smoothies

Boloco $
13 Massachusetts locations
www.boloco.com

Boloco is a hip, cheery chain dedicated to burritos and smoothies. Students line up to mix-and-match a choice of chicken, steak, or tofu with California-inspired flavors. The Bangkok burrito gets messy with Thai peanut sauce, Asian slaw, cukes, and rice; while the Caesar burrito brings it back East with creamy dressing, lettuce, feta, and herb croutons. The Cajun burrito features black beans, corn salsa, and sour cream, while the Teriyaki burrito mixes caramelized onions, broccoli, carrots, and rice. Smoothies are just as creative: enjoy flavors like Mango Passion, Berry Blitz, the Cape Codder (with cranberries), and the Jimmy Carter, made from peanut butter, bananas, and frozen yogurt.

THE GREATEST: Pizza

Papa Gino's $
129 Massachusetts locations
www.papaginos.com

Papa Gino's serves up a spectacular slice, making it Boston's most popular pizzeria. Their secret recipe involves vine-ripened tomato sauce, a three-cheese blend, and a hand-stretched thin crust. Phantom usually gets one of the specialty pies, like the chicken and roasted pepper, the spicy Buffalo chicken, or the Paparoni with twice the cheese and pepperoni. They also serve a free-form Rustic Pizza with a buttery, even thinner crust. Papa Gino's goes way beyond menu basics to offer salads, Barilla pasta dinners, cold subs, hot pockets, and grilled panini.

THE GREATEST: Wraps

Fresh City $
11 Massachusetts locations
www.FreshCity.com

Coining the term "fresh fusion," Fresh City blends a garden variety of meats, grains, and produce into wholesome tortilla bundles. It's not your average sandwich shop, featuring dishes that combine wild salmon, jasmine rice, and Dijon mustard sauce, or chicken, beans, salsa, and guacamole. The Great Caesar is basically a one-handed salad, and the Peking duck includes Beijing slaw and hoisin sauce. The wraps come hot or cold, and the menu also includes soups, noodles, stir-fry, and smoothies. Locations in Logan Airport, Boston's Landmark Center, Framingham, and Newton.

THE GREATEST: Grilled Panini

Pressed Sandwiches $
2 Oliver St., Boston, MA, (617) 482-9700
www.pressedsandwiches.com
Stock is up at Pressed Sandwiches, a hot little Financial District storefront. The artichoke-themed atmosphere is as toasty as the sandwiches themselves, grilled panini-style until they gush gooey cheese from their crusty clasp. For breakfast, there's egg and cheddar on brioche or the American in Europe with melted chocolate hazelnut spread on brioche. Lunch creations include prosciutto and fig, bresaola and fontina, or tuna and artichoke. The operation is super quick, but neighborhood suits feel right at home in this attractive setting with blackboard walls and raised stools. There's a second Pressed Sandwiches on Bedford Street and a third in the Seaport District.

THE GREATEST: Steak and Cheese

Carl's Steak Subs $
55 Prospect St., Waltham, MA, (781) 893-9313
Forget Philly; the best cheesesteaks in the country come from Carl's, where there's barely enough room for the takeout counter. Their steak bombs pack over a pound of meat made from a secret two-beef blend. There are 30 spins on the original, and many have never before been on the steak and cheese circuit. The Firecracker fuses pepperoni and tomato sauce into the mix, while the Kamikaze takes on sausage, ham, bacon, and BBQ sauce. There's also the Misteak with meatballs, sausage, mushrooms, and onion, and the Mexican spiced with hot jalapeños. Score the same steak and cheeses at their sister restaurants: Tory's in Leominster and T. C. Lando's in Acton and Hudson.

THE GREATEST: Healthy Fast Food

b.good $
131 Dartmouth St., Boston, MA, (617) 424-5252
www.bgood.com
This local favorite cuts calories with smart ingredients and grilling. Their no-fry fries are outstanding, crisped in an oven rather than dunked in the Frialator. The

b.good burger is made with lean ground beef, caramelized onions, sautéed mushrooms, and garlicky greens on a toasted Portuguese sweet roll. Fabulous shakes are mixed with nonfat frozen yogurt and fresh fruit, and sandwiches include the Buffalo chicken with blue cheese dressing and the grilled steak on a toasted baguette. There's also a Harvard Square location.

THE GREATEST: Nutritious Fast Food

O'Natural's $
83 Exchange St., Portland, ME, (207) 321-2050
www.onaturals.com

O'Natural's is pioneering a fast food revolution with all-natural snacks served lickety-split in an earthy environment that's actually inviting. They use real silverware rather than the plastic stuff, and customers can sit in leather chairs and read the newspaper. Their warm flatbread sandwiches are fabulous, like the Chicken & Roots with pesto, brie, and root veggies. The Wrangler stacks roast beef, rosemary onions, and Swiss cheese. Pizzas are loaded with fire-roasted tomato sauce, and other highlights include five-spice noodles and spicy peanut salad. O'Natural's also brings its act to Falmouth, Maine, and Acton, Massachusetts.

THE GREATEST: Old-Fashioned Fries

Al's French Frys $
1251 Williston Rd., Burlington, VT, (802) 862-9203
www.alsfrenchfrys.com

Al's French Frys is a '50s classic with checkered floors, red booths, and neon lights. The crispy, crunchy, golden twigs take the main stage, as customers watch mounds of whole russets go through the entire process of being peeled, cut, and fried. Salt, ketchup, and vinegar are stationed at every table, but the two most popular add-ons are turkey gravy and cheddar cheese sauce. Other tempting items include burgers, hot dogs, and milkshakes.

Fine Dining

GREAT ATE

THE GREATEST: **Proposal Restaurant**

L'Espalier $$$
30 Gloucester St., Boston, MA, (617) 262-3023
www.lespalier.com

L'Espalier is *the* place for popping the question. The townhouse setting is a series of intimate rooms with marble fireplaces. Famous for elaborate tasting menus featuring caviar and truffles, the French kitchen crafts dishes like pecan crusted lamb in cumin-raisin sauce. Fine desserts might include the warm chestnut and cayenne soufflé with walnut anglaise, followed by an off-the-charts cheese tray of thirty seasonal selections. L'Espalier has announced a Summer 2008 relocation to the state-of-the-art Mandarin Oriental Boston Hotel in the Prudential Center. Guests will enjoy the same exquisite cuisine amidst floor-to-ceiling windows, a glass elevator, and a chocolate exhibition room.

THE GREATEST: **Fine Dining Prix Fixe**

Craigie Street Bistrot $$$
5 Craigie Circle, Cambridge, MA, (617) 497-5511
www.craigiestreetbistrot.com

Hidden between Harvard Square and Huron Village, Craigie Street Bistrot has no end of diners capable of finding the basement-level location. Hefty prices, difficult parking, and tough reservations . . . no obstacle could deter Phantom. Once you've arrived, the quaintness of the room stretches all the way to the newspaper-covered WC. The waitstaff could pass a pop quiz on micro greens, and the hearty French fare is still trendy enough for the Cambridge clientele. Think rillettes, eggs en cocotte, pig belly with crispy sweetbreads, and rosemary-poached pears. The best deal on the clipboard menu is the $30 three-course Neighborhood Menu served Wednesday, Thursday, and Sunday, and after 9:00 p.m. on Friday and Saturday.

THE GREATEST: Roasted Chicken

Hamersley's Bistro $$$
553 Tremont St., Boston, MA, (617) 423-2700
www.hamersleysbistro.com

Hamersley's Bistro perfects fine dining in blue jeans. The French comfort food will blow your mind, with house specialties like succulent roasted chicken that surrenders garlic, lemon, and parsley in every moist, delicious bite. The New England seafood stew pulls out all the stops with calamari, clams, monkfish, and hearty pumpkin in a luxurious tomato broth, and the apple croustade envelopes cinnamon-coated apples and fresh thyme in a purse of flaky pie dough. The handsome setting feels like a country French home, but the open kitchen provides a clear shot of chef Gordon Hamersley sporting his signature Red Sox cap.

THE GREATEST: Chef's Table

Aujourd'hui $$$
Four Seasons Boston, 200 Boylston St., Boston, MA, (617) 351-2037
www.fourseasons.com/boston/dining

Aujourd'hui is worth its weight in caviar, especially for its million-dollar view of the Boston Public Garden. The luxurious dining room rolls out the red carpet in a contemporary setting of pretty floral chairs, Italian linens, and Bernaudeau china. In between the *amuse bouche* and petits fours, save room for fine French dishes like butternut squash and lobster bisque, poured into a bowl at the table. The pan-seared black sea bass is delicate and delicious served over confit eggplant and mushroom risotto. If you're going all out, reserve Table 76, where the chef prepares an outrageous four-course tasting menu paired with wines.

THE GREATEST: Rare Cuisine

Clio $$$
370 Commonwealth Ave., Boston, MA, (617) 536-7200
www.cliorestaurant.com

Clio's extreme cuisine makes for a special splurge. The wildly artistic menu reworks rare imported ingredients with food lab experiments like foams and infusions. The ingenious results are palate-challenging, like the peppered Kobe rib eye with black licorice and fig chutney. Phantom's favorite is the salmon tartare with avocado, gold beets, and red ginger. Fierce leopard-print carpets and a lattice ceiling reinforce the upscale, urban atmosphere, and chef/owner Ken Oringer can often be seen at Uni, his sashimi bar downstairs.

THE GREATEST: Splurge with a View

Spiced Pear $$$
The Chanler at Cliff Walk, 117 Memorial Blvd., Newport, RI,
(401) 847-2244
www.spicedpear.com

The Spiced Pear is a magical dining experience set in The Chanler at Cliff Walk—
a luxurious boutique hotel. The restaurant practically hangs over the water, and
there's a gorgeous veranda with a stunning view of the ocean. Inside, it feels like
one of the historic mansions of Newport. Global fusion describes the chef's tasting
menus, which are offered in three, five, or seven flights. Highlights include lobster
with sweet corn succotash and Nova Scotia halibut with langoustines and heirloom
tomato salad. The chocolate trio dessert is out of sight, culminating in a crispy
chocolate caramel bombe.

THE GREATEST: Fine Dining

Upstairs on the Square $$$
91 Winthrop St., Cambridge, MA, (617) 864-1933
www.upstairsonthesquare.com

Upstairs on the Square near Harvard has two floors of eye-catching décor with animal-
print carpeting, eclectic chandeliers, and '40s panache. The opulent Soirée Room is a
peach vision of metallic brushstrokes and fireplaces, while the Monday Club Bar features mint green walls, a purple-and-pink checkered floor, and a fuchsia porch. It's fine
dining without a financial doubt, but totally fun with touches like Twizzlers for bar
snacks. The eclectic menu is bold, featuring dishes like the caramelized Berkshire
pork chop with mustard gnocchi and ice wine. They also do a fabulous Sunday brunch
with specialties like duck confit hash, brioche French toast, and lobster omelets.

THE GREATEST: Understated Elegance

Seasons $$$
Millennium Bostonian Hotel, 26 North St., Boston, MA, (617) 523-4119
www.millenniumhotels.com/boston

Seasons in the Millennium Bostonian Hotel is a natural celebration venue with an
understated, elegant atmosphere. A draped-cloth ceiling and well-spaced tables
produce an impeccable setting with plenty of privacy. All eyes are on the elevated
view of the Faneuil Hall Marketplace and the city skyline. Both the extensive
American wine list and the New American cuisine stand out on the menu, with
dishes like molasses duck breast and shiitake dusted cod. Visual presentation is im-
pressive, with many dishes towering vertically or blazing with color.

Food and Fun
GREAT ATE

THE GREATEST: Restaurant from the Future

LTK $$

225 Northern Ave., Boston, MA, (617) 330-7430

www.ltkbarandkitchen.com

Short for "Legal Test Kitchen," LTK is a hotbed of innovation in both the dining room and the kitchen. The exciting, affordable menu has quite a range from Haitian chicken wings to grilled shrimp nachos. The incredible wok omelet is cooked with chicken, shrimp, and sweet chili sauce, and the Big Pancake is really a personal-sized Bundt cake drenched in maple syrup. The dining room is just as cutting edge. Servers are armed with wireless handheld computers that transmit orders directly to the kitchen. Customers can surf the web, watch TV, or play with an iPod docking station.

THE GREATEST: Dinner Cruise

Odyssey Cruises $$$

Rowes Wharf at Boston Harbor Hotel, (866) 307-2469

www.odysseycruises.com/boston

Setting sail aboard the Odyssey is the ultimate escape for a romantic evening. It's a little pricey, but the package includes three hours of dining, live music and dancing, and an incredible view the entire time. The observation deck is ideal for drinking in the sunset, but be sure to save room for the four-course feast. Hors d'oeuvres like whipped basil feta kick off the meal followed by rich lobster cobbler, beef Wellington, or stuffed chicken breast. The ship photographer takes everyone's picture, and you can arrange for a bottle of bubbly to be waiting at your table. Odyssey sets sail for brunch and lunch.

THE GREATEST: Sports Bar

Game On! $$

82 Lansdowne St., Boston, MA, (617) 351-7001

www.gameonboston.com

Game On! is a surround-sound playground where the sports fan comes first. The massive, two-level space fits 500 people. Upstairs there's outdoor seating, but downstairs every available inch is filled with high-definition televisions and plasma screens. If your game isn't on one of the main screens above the bar, you can reserve a private skybox and watch any team you want. The food at Game On! goes way beyond typical pub grub. Try the massive "nacho experience" loaded with chicken and all the fixings. Fresh-cut fries are covered in cheddar, sour cream, and bacon, and the rest of the bases are covered with lobster rolls, steak tips, and hot dogs smothered with chili and cheese.

THE GREATEST: Dinner and Gaming

Kings Restaurant $$
10 Scotia St., Boston, MA, (617) 266-2695
www.backbaykings.com

Kings, housed in the Back Bay's former Cheri theater, is a nightlifer's playground of bowling, billiards, video games, and lounge dining. Sixteen black-lit big-ball bowling lanes rock the hot modern scene, along with funky shoes and automatic scoring computers that also let you order drinks. For late-night (or brunch or lunch) noshing, there's a retro lounge serving scintillating cocktails like the Big Ball Bowl. Eclectic American cuisine ranges from thin-crust pizza to seafood and comfort food like steak and fries.

THE GREATEST: Interactive Dining

Fire + Ice $$
50 Church St., Cambridge, MA, (617) 547-9007
www.fire-ice.com

Fire + Ice in Cambridge, the Back Bay, and Providence is a colorful, quirky "interactive dining experience." It's an all-you-can-eat bonanza where customers hand-pick their meal from a giant spread of seafood, chicken, lamb, turkey, steak, forty kinds of veggies, and noodles. After selecting one of ten sauces like Zesty Pomodoro, Sweet Chili, or Fajita, the grill chefs stir-fry the whole thing at an enormous grill right in the middle of the dining room. Customers are entertained by spatula tricks before they get their sizzling hot grub, head back to their table, and stuff it into warm tortillas or pile it on top of rice.

THE GREATEST: Fun First Date

Ascari Café at F1 Boston $$
290 Wood Rd., Braintree, MA, (781) 848-2300
www.f1boston.com

Ladies and gentlemen, rev your engines! F1 Boston is Phantom's favorite pit stop *and* first date destination. At the area's only indoor go-kart racetrack, you can work up an appetite for pub grub (and love) while zipping into a red jumpsuit and matching helmet. Phantom likes to order nachos and burgers at the trackside Ascari Café while strategizing over the next go round. They also have a full bar for post-race cocktails. Pictures of famous drivers help break the ice and fuel conversation while you're placing bets about the cars below. Phantom suggests racing before you eat, since a big dinner can weigh you down in the fast lane.

THE GREATEST: No-Rules Restaurant

10 Prime Steak & Sushi $$$
55 Pine St., Providence, RI, (401) 453-2333
www.tenprimesteakandsushi.com

At 10 Prime Steak & Sushi, USDA Prime beef meets wild, sexy sushi. Phantom enjoys sipping a glowing martini over savory appetizers like lobster Rangoon with apricot Thai dipping sauce. The potent juice-filled Scorpion Bowl arrives in flames. There's even a whopping 40-ounce porterhouse steak; anyone crazy enough to finish it gets a plaque. The atmosphere breaks as many rules as the food, with an "underwater" dining room and a 3-D dessert menu. Try Cheryl's Wedding Cake, which is so darn tall it requires a steak knife to keep it upright. This isn't just dining, it's eat-ertainment.

THE GREATEST: Fondue

The Melting Pot $$
92 Worcester Rd., Framingham, MA, (508) 875-3115
www.themeltingpot.com

The Melting Pot is a fondue chain that has finally bubbled up near Boston. The menu includes five cheese, four broth, and nine chocolate fondues. Most are prepared tableside by servers who stir and season each concoction, like the traditional Swiss cheese with white wine and garlic. There's also a spicy Mexican mix of cheddar, jalapeños, and salsa. All-you-can-eat bread, veggies, and apples are served on the side, and upgrades include shrimp, lobster, or filet mignon. For dessert, there's an over-the-top Yin & Yang fondue swirling dark and white chocolate with dippers like brownies, fruit, cheesecake, and Oreo-covered marshmallows.

French Fries
GREAT ATE

THE GREATEST: Belgian Fries

Duckfat $$
43 Middle St., Portland, ME, (207) 774-8080
www.duckfat.com

Part watering hole, part upscale sandwich shack, Duckfat is a colorful hangout that's 100 percent delicious. Their signature Belgian fries are fried in duck fat, resulting in a crunchy, airy, insanely addictive snack. They're served the Belgian way, in a paper cone and accompanied by homemade condiments like truffle ketchup, horseradish mayo, curry mayo, and duck gravy. The comfort food menu also includes grilled panini sandwiches, "five-dollar" milkshakes, and fresh donut holes dipped in powdered sugar. Customers can pass the wait crafting magnetic poetry on the wall.

THE GREATEST: Train Wreck Fries

Ashmont Grill $$
555 Talbot Ave., Dorchester, MA, (617) 825-4300
www.ashmontgrill.com

The Ashmont Grill is a pretty stylish neighborhood spot, but Phantom would criss-cross the city for their Train Wreck Fries. These hand-cut, skin-on spuds come smothered in jack cheese, sour cream, applewood-smoked bacon, scallions, and hot jalapeños. Hanging blackboard menus list everything from chicken pesto pizza to the River Rock Burger with grilled onions on a grilled bun. The baked mac and cheese overloads on three kinds of cheese plus sun-dried tomatoes, and there's even a banana split for dessert. When the weather heats up, outdoor seating sprawls across the sidewalk and back patio.

THE GREATEST: Blue Cheese Fries

B-Side Lounge $$
92 Hampshire St., Cambridge, MA, (617) 354-0766
www.bsidelounge.com

B-Side Lounge cooks the most imaginative bar food, and their decadent blue cheese fries are no exception. They're rich and salty, with real blue cheese that's chunky but melted; the massive mess feeds four people. Other specialties include baked Gouda in a skillet, the Buffalo shrimp po'boy, and chocolate port fondue served with pound cake, toffee, strawberries, and dried fruit. The retro atmosphere falls somewhere between funky diner and neighborhood watering hole, and the wrap-around bar features cans of Schlitz and forgotten cocktails like the Sidecar. Free bar snacks include hard-boiled eggs!

THE GREATEST: Poutine

Harvest $$$
44 Brattle St., Cambridge, MA, (617) 868-2255
www.the-harvest.com
What do you get when you cross cheese, french fries, gravy, and scallions? A serious snack attack! Poutine is a delicious mess that's practically the national dish of Canada. But you don't have to cross the border to sample it; Harvest offers an authentic version on their bar menu. Shoestring fries are dotted with cheese curds, baked until gooey, and then drizzled with chicken gravy. The whole thing is topped with scallions and served with an entire stack of napkins. Inside, Harvest resembles an intimate country club. The kitchen's modern American specialties include lobster bisque with sunchoke chips, and Kurobuta pork with glazed chestnuts and cider cream.

THE GREATEST: Curly Fries

Coolidge Corner Clubhouse $$
307 Harvard St., Brookline, MA, (617) 566-4948
Affectionately known as the "CCC," Coolidge Corner Clubhouse is the perfect place to watch a game and sip some suds. Athlete-named dishes like the Cam Neely Burger come with a side of curly fries so absurdly gigantic it's almost impossible to find the entrée underneath. In fact, it's one of the only restaurants where Phantom requests a doggie bag. Every day there's a sports trivia question on the menu board, and anyone who answers correctly (no cell phones or Internet access allowed) gets a free slice of chocolate mud pie.

THE GREATEST: Gravy Fries

Deluxe Town Diner $
627 Mt. Auburn St., Watertown, MA, (617) 926-8400
Deluxe Town Diner is an expanded 1930s Worcester dining car, completely restored with porcelain blue tiles, vinyl booths, and neon lights. Their upscale diner food includes Phantom's favorite gravy fries, better known as "Wets." Hand-cut spuds are cooked to a sink-your-teeth-into state poised between crunchy and tender, and slathered with meaty gravy. Other gourmet blue plate specials include the all-natural Kobe beef burger, apple crumb pie with vanilla bean ice cream, and sweet potato pancakes.

THE GREATEST: **Bottomless Fries**

Red Robin $$
Locations in Plymouth and Millbury
www.redrobin.com

Any place that offers bottomless fries deserves accolade in Phantom's purple book. When you buy a burger at Red Robin, it comes with an endless supply of their fat steak fries. But don't fill up on all that starch—the adventurous burgers come in 20-plus flavors that think way outside the bun. They range from the classic cheeseburger to the Royal Red Robin topped with a fresh fried egg. The Banzai is marinated in teriyaki and layered with grilled pineapple, while the Guacamole Bacon features succulent hickory-smoked rashers. They even have "Knife and Forkers" like the Burger Parmigiana finished with marinara and crispy fried mozzarella.

THE GREATEST: **Suzie Q Potato**

Skip's Snack Bar $
92 East Main St., Merrimac, MA, (978) 346-8686

There are thousands of ways to slice a spud, but no one does it quite like Skip's Snack Bar. Since 1947, this Merrimac mainstay has cranked out millions of pounds of their signature Suzie Q Potato. Shaped like a spiral phone cord, the curly Suzie Q has been made the same way, on the same hand-powered slicers, for 60 years. While most of the curls are eight inches long, the record is a whopping 16 feet, made from one giant spud. The '50s-themed quick stop makes other fast food, too: grilled hot dogs, turkey clubs, and chicken fingers. But Phantom's favorite is the Angus beef double cheeseburger.

Fried Clams
GREAT ATE

THE GREATEST: **Original Fried Clam**

Woodman's of Essex $$
121 Main St. (Rte. 133), Essex, MA, (978) 768-6057
www.woodmans.com

Woodman's of Essex is a mecca of the fried clam world, and it's also the alleged inventor of the fried mollusk. In 1916, Lawrence "Chubby" Woodman took the meat out of the steamers, tossed it in the fryer, and never looked back. Whether that's a myth or a part of bivalve history, no other clam shack comes close to Woodman's tender, plump clam in a light fried batter. Woodman's also sells the best onion rings Phantom has ever eaten, as well as steamed lobster that customers handpick outside. Eat in a rustic wooden booth or on the back lawn overlooking the lush marsh.

THE GREATEST: **Ipswich Clams**

J. T. Farnham's $$
88 Eastern Ave. (Rte. 133), Essex, MA, (978) 768-6643

J. T. Farnham's makes a righteous case for using sweet, succulent Ipswich clams. Their rich, soft shells are local delicacies from the nearby muddy flats. With lots of down-home charm, it's a scenic setting of picnic tables positioned over the Essex Salt Marsh. Inside, the full-bellied critters take a dip in egg wash and corn flour and emerge from the Frialator with a delicate, crunchy coating. That hot, golden garb dissolves instantaneously on the tongue, releasing scrumptious savory flavor.

THE GREATEST: **Clam Cakes**

Harraseeket Lunch $$
Town Landing South Main St., Freeport, ME, (207) 865-3535

At Harraseeket Lunch, the dive-bombing seagulls are a testament to how delicious the clam cakes are. These soft, golden patties contain briny bits of bivalve with an irresistibly chewy texture. Other house specialties include boiled lobster, fried seafood baskets, and breaded golden onion middles. Located on the town wharf, this seafood shanty even does a darn good dessert course, including roly-poly whoopie pies. The BYOB policy contributes to a shockingly inexpensive meal.

THE GREATEST: Clam Strips

Kream N' Kone $
961 Main St. (Rte. 28), West Dennis, MA, (508) 394-0808
www.kreamnkone.com
Kream N' Kone is a Cape Cod favorite with legendary fried seafood like Phantom's favorite clam strips. Without the messy whole bellies (which some people don't like), all that's left is the wonderfully tender neck. The necks are cooked to a gorgeous 14-karat color with just enough chew. Kream N' Kone offers seven kinds of seafood rolls, outstanding onion rings, and 24 flavors of soft serve. Their modern, air-conditioned location sits right on Swan River.

THE GREATEST: Batter-Fried Clams

Red Wing $$
Rte. 1 South, Walpole, MA, (508) 668-0453
Red Wing is a landlocked Worcester dining car where the fried clams are so famous, seaside dwellers make the reverse commute here. The kitchen uses plump Ipswich bivalves and a minimum amount of batter, so the true clam taste comes through, hot and juicy with salty bursts of the sea exploding in your mouth. For a smaller catch, Phantom loves the broiled scallops, the classic lobster roll, and the creamy clam chowder. Red Wing also does one heck of a bar pie pizza.

THE GREATEST: Clam Shack

The Clam Box $$
246 High St., Ipswich, MA, (978) 356-9707
The Clam Box is one of the great restaurant wonders of the world, constructed to look like an actual takeout box. (If Phantom could order a box of their clams that big, he would!) Their native fried clams are legendary, all crisp and crunchy without any heavy grease. The kitchen changes the frying oil every few hours so the briny mollusks are always caramel colored and lightly sweet. Orders can be solo, but the Caped Critic gets his on a plate loaded with onion rings and fries. The fisherman's platter adds haddock, jumbo shrimp, and scallops to the deep-fried mix.

THE GREATEST: Breaded Fried Clams

Hingham Lobster Pound $$
4 Broad Cove Rd. (Rte. 3A), Hingham, MA, (781) 749-1984
Once a bait shop, Hingham Lobster Pound is now a takeout clam shack that has Nantasket beachgoers swerving off of 3A for their breaded fried clams. Many seafood specialists find flour to be a lighter, cheaper alternative, but the Pound

spares no expense to create a second skin of blistering crunch over each briny full-bellied clam. The onion rings crackle with the same fried coating, and the banana fritters melt in your mouth. Nostalgic pictures of Hingham and Nantasket cover the ordering galley, and customers can quiz themselves with Trivial Pursuit cards while waiting. Call ahead two hours for steamed lobster.

THE GREATEST: Fisherman's Platter

The Lobster Pot   **$$**
3155 Cranberry Hwy., East Wareham, MA, (508) 759-3876
The Lobster Pot is a Cape Cod favorite with spectacular fried seafood. Their fisherman's platter brims with lightly battered seafood, the only issue being whether the scallops are better than the clams. Enjoy your deliberations: they're all crispy, crunchy, and delicious. They have excellent clam rolls and strips, too. Believe it or not, they take special orders for fresh lobsters at up to 20 whopping pounds! There's actually a guy from New York who flies here every year just to eat one of these monster shellfish before flying directly home. A fresh seafood market is also on the premises.

Guilty Pleasures
GREAT ATE

THE GREATEST: Fried Dough

Blink's Fry Doe $
115 Ocean Blvd., Hampton Beach, NH, (603) 926-4887
Blink's bright orange shack on the Hampton Beach boardwalk is a beacon for fried dough fanatics. The dough is made by hand every day, following a top-secret recipe. Beyond the usual sugar and cinnamon toppings, their mind-boggling menu lists 20 flavors. Phantom's favorites include peanut butter and jelly, honey and walnuts, sauce and cheese, butter and garlic, and coconut. The truly adventurous can create new combinations like peanut butter and chocolate, and fruit fans can choose from raspberry, blueberry, strawberry, or apple cinnamon.

THE GREATEST: Chocolate-Dipped Fruit

Chocolate Dipper $
Chestnut Hill Mall, 199 Boylston St., Chestnut Hill, MA, (617) 969-7252
www.thechocolatedipper.com
The Chocolate Dipper specializes in chocolate-dipped fresh fruit. Their extravagant assortment includes jumbo glazed Australian apricots, kiwi slices, blueberries, green grapes, raspberries, bananas, and the ever-popular strawberry. Aside from fruit, the Dipper offers chocolate-dipped cookies, pretzels, truffles, caramels, nuts, and brownies. Luscious milk chocolate is mixed in 100-pound tanks, and skilled chocolatiers prepare these premium goodies in full view of the customer. They have another location at Downtown Crossing.

THE GREATEST: Fried Chicken

Coast Café $
233 River St., Cambridge, MA, (617) 354-7644
This teeny tiny takeout spot serves up golden fried chicken so good, it could resuscitate Colonel Sanders. Every piece is crispy and juicy, each bite fully seasoned to the bone. There are falling-off-the-bone ribs, hearty meatloaf sandwiches, and grilled chicken. And, of course, a proper Southern dinner isn't complete without comfort food sides like mac and cheese and sweet candied yams. Desserts are as rich and delicious as the rest, including sweet potato pie, brownies, and chocolate chip cookies as big as dinner plates. Their greatest guilty pleasure is the creamy banana pudding, layered over sliced bananas and vanilla cookies.

THE GREATEST: Cream-Filled Donuts

Butler's Colonial Donut House $
459 Sanford Rd., Westport, MA, (508) 672-4600

For 50 years, Butlers has made the best cream-filled donuts on the planet. The fluffy yeast dough is sliced through the middle and filled with silky smooth whipped cream, resulting in a dream dessert that's light as a cloud and soft as a pillow. Butler's is known for a second specialty: the Long John. Made from the same airy dough and decadent cream, this sub-shaped pastry includes a ribbon of sweet black raspberry jelly. Rounding out the sugary offerings are chocolate-glazed donuts, apple-spice donuts, cherry tarts, and apple fritters.

THE GREATEST: Cannoli Selection

Wholly Cannoli $
488 Grafton St., Worcester, MA, (508) 753-0224
www.whollycannoli.com

With more than 20 flavors, Wholly Cannoli claims to have the largest cannoli assortment on the entire East Coast. The traditional Italian recipe has a crispy shell and sweet ricotta filling, but Wholly Cannoli specializes in unusual flavors like citrus, peanut butter, pumpkin, and mint chocolate chip. The chocolate amaretto cannoli has a Florentine shell and piña colada filling, and the banana split cannoli is bursting with ripe fruit flavor. Their most explosive offering is the Dynamite Stick: a crunchy chocolate shell fluffed full of rich ricotta and gooey caramel.

THE GREATEST: Nuts

Fastachi $
598 Mt. Auburn St., Watertown, MA, (617) 924-8787
www.fastachi.com

Fastachi has a knack for nuts, which they roast in a steel drum and mix in small, flavorful batches. Sea salt brings out the character of each whole nut before they're blended into snack attack combinations like their signature cranberry-nut mix with pistachios, almonds, hazelnuts, sesame peanuts, and cashews. Hot-and-sour wasabi is more exotic; the fruit passion mix is bursting with dried apricots, pears, papaya, and sour cherries. There's also the PB&J mix, nailing the flavors of the sandwich with roasted peanuts and dried cranberries. All of the ensembles are displayed in the store like a snack buffet, sold alongside marzipan fruits and tiramisu chocolate truffles.

THE GREATEST: **Cream Puffs**

Beard Papa's $
1 Faneuil Hall Marketplace, Boston, MA, (617) 570-9070
www.muginohousa.com

Beard Papa's is a Japanese chain making the world's best cream puffs. Quincy Market customers can watch the treats as they're assembled on the spot. The puffs start with choux pastry baked in a special two-layer shell that's crispy on the outside and soft inside. The puffs are filled to order and finished with powdered sugar. Whipped vanilla custard made from Madagascar vanilla beans is Beard Papa's signature, but additional flavors include Belgian chocolate and strawberry. They can also be piped into a chocolate-covered éclair.

THE GREATEST: **Flavored Fries**

Sunset Grill & Tap $$
130 Brighton Ave., Allston, MA, (617) 254-1331
www.allstonsfinest.com

Any place that serves more than 500 beers *must* serve good pub grub. Sunset's half-pound burgers are cooked on a steam grill to seal in the flavors and juices. As for the fries, the quality curly fries come to the table in a gigantic basket that easily serves 10 monster appetites. The fries are addictive in their own right, but they're even better topped with sour cream and chives or spicy Cajun fire. For the ultimate spud spree, check out the Green Monster potato skins with pesto chicken strips, roasted red peppers, and mozzarella.

Hidden Jewels
GREAT ATE

THE GREATEST: Gangster Wraps

The Real Deal $
1882 Centre St., West Roxbury, MA, (617) 325-0754

The Real Deal is like a sandwich shop on steroids. The prices are real low, the place real busy, and the menu real big. With 100 items, customers enjoy options from sandwiches and burgers to wings and Buffalo chicken pizza. "Gangster" wraps are named after famous mobsters, and it's no surprise that the Godfather gets the most hits with a winning combination of corned beef, turkey, and Russian dressing. The "hot off the press" paninis include the Carmella Soprano with roasted eggplant. As for "monster" burgers, the King Kong storms the bun with blue cheese, onion rings, and hot sauce.

THE GREATEST: Movie-Themed Diner

The Breakfast Club $
270 Western Ave., Allston, MA, (617) 783-1212

Fans of the classic '80s movie will recognize the name, but anyone who appreciates a great morning meal will love The Breakfast Club. Set in an authentic Worcester diner with red vinyl booths, the place offers "library specials" named after characters from the flick. The Dork serves a small appetite with two eggs and home fries, while the Criminal adds a side of crispy bacon or corned beef hash. The Princess is a hot Belgian waffle loaded with fresh fruit and whipped cream, and the lean Jock features scrambled egg whites with veggies and wheat toast. Finally, there's the gigantic Basket Case of eggs, sausage, home fries, and thick French toast.

THE GREATEST: BBQ Pit Master

Pit Stop Barbeque $
888 Morton St., Boston, MA, (617) 436-0485

Pit Stop Barbeque is so tightly spaced that customers can hardly see through the take-out window. It's cramped to the point that the grill master has to sit on the floor. The cash register is on one side, the prep area is on the other, and the middle houses an old-fashioned brick pit where the seated cook tends to mouth-watering ribs, sausage, and chicken. The meaty menu has all the BBQ staples plus side dishes like candied yams, collard greens, mac and cheese, and sweet potato pie.

THE GREATEST: Old-School Pizzeria

The New Brown Jug $
24 Adams St., Chelsea, MA, (617) 884-9579
www.newbrownjug.com

The New Brown Jug is an old-school pizzeria with one of the best daily specials around: a cheese pizza and a pitcher of beer for less than $13. It's such a great value, there's a limit to one per table. The two-person pies feature gooey cheese on a thin, floppy slice with crackly, brittle edges. Increase the crust by ordering a "double dough." Phantom's favorite is topped with bacon and meatballs, and The Jug also does a darn good calzone, particularly the pork with vinegar peppers and the "Jake's Steak" stuffed with shredded beef, peppers, onions, and red pepper spice.

THE GREATEST: Rock 'n' Roll Restaurant

5 & Diner $
525 Lincoln St., Worcester, MA, (508) 852-6100
www.5anddiner.com

The 5 & Diner is a national chain that's covered in so much '50s memorabilia, it could pass as a bebop museum. Waitresses wear coin changers and nametags like "The Fonz" while delivering humongous portions of comfort food. Phantom's favorite is the double-decker Big Bopper Burger, but there's also a Cobb salad that could feed a family of four. The biggest and most popular item is the Cadillac Meatloaf, served in thick slices topped with bacon, mushrooms, and crispy onion straws. They also do the most decadent hot dog Phantom has ever eaten: stuffed and topped with cheese, wrapped in bacon, and served on a grilled buttered bun.

THE GREATEST: Creative Breakfast

Arthur & Pat's $
239 Ocean St., Marshfield, MA, (781) 834-9755

Arthur & Pat's flips and folds Phantom's favorite omelets, like the lobster specialty with seafood, spinach, and cheese sauce. Their biggest strength lies in 26 years of family-run tradition combined with overflowing menu creativity from the chef. Two hundred selections are posted all over the walls in a mouth-watering collage. The potato pancakes are topped with smoked salmon and poached eggs, and kids go crazy for the banana Belgian waffle with warm vanilla bean sauce and glazed pecans. Arthur & Pat's is only open seasonally from April to October.

THE GREATEST: Cheesesteak

Moogy's $
154 Chestnut Hill Ave., Brighton, MA, (617) 254-8114
www.moogys.com
Moogy's is a funky storefront where college kids grab some grub, challenge each
other to board games, and relax with a beer. It's no place for health nuts, but Phantom loves their extensive menu of authentic Philly cheesesteaks. The basic blends
two kinds of beef with provolone and American. But the Caped Critic's favorite is
undoubtedly the Phantom Royal with Cheese. It's stuffed with onion rings and
smothered with BBQ sauce. Moogy's offers a dozen chicken steaks, rarities like the
Reuben burger and the pizza burger, and breakfast all day.

THE GREATEST: Mixed Ice Cream

England's MicroCreamery $
109 Washington St., Haverhill, MA, (978) 373-6400
www.MicroCreamery.com
Putting a creamy twist on the microbrewery, England's MicroCreamery makes its
own small batches of ice cream on site. Each flavor is smooth, without any pre-
mixed chunks, chips, or swirls. The customer is given complete control over what
kinds of candy, cookies, and nuts are hand-folded into the scoops. If you need a little guidance, try suggested combinations like Peanut Butter & Jelly with nutty ice
cream and a raspberry swirl. Children go crazy for Willy Wonka's Schnazzberry
chock-full of Gummie Bears, and Big Daddy improves on a creamy vanilla cup
with chocolate-covered pretzels with swirls of peanut butter and chocolate.

Hot Dog
GREAT ATE

THE GREATEST: All-Beef Wiener

Spike's Junk Yard Dogs $
108 Brighton Ave., Allston, MA, (617) 254-7700
www.spikesjunkyarddogs.com
A junkyard may not be your first stop for good eats, but Spike's storefront is a haven for hot dogs. The 100 percent all-beef wieners are a special recipe made exclusively for Spike's, and the quality continues with oversized French rolls baked in-house. Phantom likes the Texas Ranger loaded with BBQ sauce, cheddar, and bacon. The Buffalo is slathered with hot sauce, blue cheese, and scallions, and the German Shepherd piles on sauerkraut and mustard. The top canine is Spike's original Junkyard Dog, wearing sliced tomato, pickles, mustard, scallions, and pepperoncini. The local chain has 10 other locations including Davis Square and Boylston Street in Boston.

THE GREATEST: Foot-Long

Grumpy White's $$
211 Sea St., Quincy, MA, (617) 770-2835
www.grumpywhites.com
At Grumpy White's, the foot-long hot dog isn't just any link; it's superior all-beef Pearl brand, served with a side of homemade mac and cheese. Every table gets a piping-hot, 18-inch loaf of fresh baked bread with a big stick of butter. Then it's on to appetizers like an extra-cheesy crock of French onion soup or golden beer battered shrimp. The overstuffed lobster roll is mixed with Hellmann's Mayonnaise, and the bacon cheeseburger served on toasted garlic bread could improve the mood of anyone . . . even Grumpy himself.

THE GREATEST: Variety

New England Hot Dog Company $
Locations in Everet and Taunton, MA, and Rindge, NH
www.nehotdog.com
New England Hot Dog Company gives the humble weenie a gourmet makeover with 50 toppings and a dozen different links like all-beef kosher, pork & beef, burgerdogs, and footlongs. From kielbasa to natural casings, the toppings range from yellow mustard and sauerkraut to pizza sauce, ranch dressing, and jalapeño

ketchup. If one just isn't enough, the Boston Beantown Dinner offers two hot dogs covered in baked beans, plus coleslaw and brown bread. Or if you want something rich, the Cambridge Bratwurst piles on the red pepper relish, Grey Poupon, and sauerkraut. Corn dogs and dirty fries are doggone delicious, and there's a "Dog Pound" play area for kids.

THE GREATEST: Toppings

Boston Speed Dog $
Newmarket Square, (Opposite Grangier Supply), Roxbury, MA
Boston Speed Dog wheels its humble cart to a busy corner in Newmarket Square, but it may offer the best hot dog in America. The Speed Dog starts as a giant half-pound all-beef Pearl brand hot dog. It's marinated in apple juice and brown sugar and grilled over scorching hot charcoal. Then, homemade toppings launch it into hot dog heaven. Mustard, sweet relish, and all-beef chili are excellent options. But Phantom opts for Speed's special sauce: a secret blend containing orange zest and grape jelly. Boston Speed Dog is open from 11 a.m. to 7 p.m. Tuesday through Friday, weather permitting.

THE GREATEST: Chili Dog

Simco's on the Bridge $$
1509 Blue Hill Ave., Mattapan, MA, (617) 296-3800
Simco's on the Bridge isn't the prettiest take-out stand, but the four-window shack sells the best foot-long dogs around. Pearl Kountry Klub links extend off a griddle-fried bun so it doesn't get soggy, and the snappy casings are topped by mustard, relish, onions, and more. The chili cheese dog is perfectly messy with greasy beans and melted American hidden underneath. But 12-inchers aren't the only thing to eat here; the fast food menu continues with pizza, seafood, onion rings, Greek lamb gyros, and hot fudge sundaes.

THE GREATEST: Condiments

Super Duper Weenie $
306 Black Rock Tpke. Fairfield, CT, (203) 334-DOGS
www.superduperweenie.com
A great, easy snack shack between Boston and NYC, Super Duper Weenie sells split-open hot dogs grilled until crispy and plump. Their fresh-cut shoestring fries are the ideal accessory to a satisfying fast food meal. These long, bronzed twigs are perfectly thin, with a hefty dousing of salt and pepper. All of the condiments are made from scratch, including sweet and hot relish, sauerkraut, chili, and onion sauce. Also on the sizzling menu are hamburgers, sausage, cheesesteak, and grilled chicken.

THE GREATEST: Gourmet Toppings

Top Dog of Rockport $
2 Doyles Cove Rd., Rockport, MA, (978) 546-0006
www.topdogrockport.com

Top Dog is a tasty little shack that serves plump, juicy wieners with condiment pizzazz. This comfy, rustic, wood-lined joint offers a great view of the water. The menu lists more than a dozen hot dog creations, grilled or steamed but always loaded with sloppy toppings like coleslaw, Vidalia onion, carrot relish, bacon, jalapeño peppers, and Boston baked beans. On the side, the Onion Brick is a condensed loaf of fried onion strings that makes for a fun peel-and-eat treat.

THE GREATEST: Dog with "The Works"

George's Coney Island Hot Dogs $
158 Southbridge St., Worcester, MA, (508) 753-4362
www.georgesconeyisland.com

From the 60-foot neon hot dog sign to the graffiti walls carved with customers' names, George's Coney Island is a historic hot dog landmark. The art-deco design features wooden booths, tile floors, and a stool-lined counter. Since 1918, they've been grilling pork-and-beef wieners served in steamed buns. The links are small and tasty, the perfect blend of sweet and spicy. The most popular Coney Island "Up" is a hot dog with "the works," including mustard, secret recipe chili sauce, and chopped onions.

Huge Portions
GREAT ATE

THE GREATEST: Gigantic Burger

Eagle's Deli & Restaurant $
1918 Beacon St., Brighton, MA, (617) 731-3232

Eagle's Deli is a hole-in-the-wall grill with one heck of a he-man burger. If you thought their three-pound Reilly burger was a beast, the five-pounder will blow your expectations clear off the bun. Piled with 10 half-pound patties, the sky-high stacking is held together by a wooden teriyaki stick. It includes 20 strips of bacon, 20 slices of cheese, and 5 pounds of fries. Finish the whole think in under an hour, and you'll get your money back ($100!) and the burger named after you. The deli also cooks up awesome corned beef and turkey tips.

THE GREATEST: All-You-Can-Eat Lobster

Nordic Lodge $$$
178 East Pasquisset Trail, Charlestown, RI, (401) 783-4515
www.nordic-lodge.com

The Nordic Lodge is home of the legendary Giant Viking Buffet. For $70 per person, this all-you-can-eat blowout features lobster, lobster, and more lobster. Seriously, they won't stop you, so long as you're within your two-hour mealtime window. The average customer cracks into a half-dozen hard bodies in a single sitting. Other high-end foods include shrimp, scallops, and juicy prime rib. There's a fried food bar, a raw bar and, for those who don't quit, a Häagen-Dazs ice cream bar. Just be sure to eat up while you can; the ban on doggie bags is strictly enforced.

THE GREATEST: Three-Pound Pizza

Sal's Pizza & Italian Restaurant $
354 Merrimack St., Lawrence, MA, (978) 291-0220
www.sals-pizza.com

Home of the 19-inch, 3-pound pizza, Sal's serves everything oversized. The plain cheese has a thick, doughy crust, and loaded specialties like the Meat Lover's can double or triple the weight. Customers with smaller appetites can order by the slice, but each extra-wide cut is one-quarter of the entire pizza. Slices are priced proportionally to the whole pie, so you won't be overcharged for "under"-ordering. Sal's isn't just about quantity; their top-notch ingredients include homemade meatballs and made-from-scratch sausage. Customize your pie with 38 toppings like shaved steak, shrimp, bacon, and blue cheese.

THE GREATEST: Colossal Coffee Roll

Kane's Donuts $
120 Lincoln Ave., Saugus, MA, (781) 233-8499
Kane's Donuts is a mom-and-pop shop making delicious donuts. The specialty of the house is their Colossal Coffee Roll, measuring 12 whopping inches across! It's loaded with cinnamon and homemade frosting and, at the size of a dinner plate, it can feed an entire family. Every one of their plump donuts is homemade and hand cut, with varieties including jelly-filled, plain, sweet-glazed, and a hot-honey-dipped. Kane's is also one of the few places that still makes the Bismark, filled with black raspberry jam and topped with fresh whipped cream.

THE GREATEST: Ice Cream Pyramid

Cabot's $
743 Washington St., Newtonville, MA, (617) 964-9200
www.cabots.com
Cabot's is a magical malt shop that overflows with ice cream sodas, frappes, freezes, floats, and parfaits. Their encyclopedic menu features 70 flavors (using Richardson's ice cream) along with frozen yogurt, as well as 30 different toppings. The biggest belly-buster is the 60-pint Great Pyramid Sundae made with 12 quarts of toppings, marshmallows, nuts, and cherries. Served like a buffet, it feeds nearly 200 people. As for individual desserts, Cabot's works its ice cream into puff pastry shells, over Belgian waffles, and around banana splits.

THE GREATEST: Family-Style Pasta

Maggiano's Little Italy $$
4 Columbus Ave., Boston, MA, (617) 542-3456
www.maggianos.com
Maggiano's Little Italy is a welcoming Italian chain where no one leaves hungry. You haven't seen family-style until you've ordered their huge plates of pasta and Italian American entrées. Half portions are available, but Phantom likes to rally the troops for an overflowing feast of gnocchi in vodka sauce, linguini with clams, and spaghetti with meatballs. They do the classics especially well, like fried calamari, veal Parmigiana, and chicken piccata. The gigantic portions are so satisfying, you'll be singing Sinatra all the way home, doggy bag in hand.

THE GREATEST: **Bottomless Grill**

Midwest Grill $$
1122 Cambridge St., Cambridge, MA, (617) 354-7536
www.midwestgrill.com

The Midwest Grill is a protein paradise featuring a bottomless pit of Brazilian rodizio-style meats and sausages. Servers skip from table to table armed with swords of meat hot off the grill. There's quite a variety, including lamb, pork tenderloin, sirloin, and chicken hearts, and customers can keep going until they're completely satisfied. The all-you-can-eat feast is supplemented by a buffet of salads, rice, beans, and potatoes; an ice cream bar serves as dessert.

THE GREATEST: **Huge Slices, Small Prices**

Ernesto's $
69 Salem St., Boston, MA, (617) 523-1373
www.ernestosnorthend.com

Anyone stopping by Ernesto's had better bring an appetite. Even if you order by the slice, it's still one-quarter of an 18-inch pie! A single slice is too big to fit on a plate. Two dozen slices are always on display, with winning combos like chicken ranch pizza that blends bacon, tomatoes, and ranch dressing. The top-selling slice is packed with chicken, pepperoni, and ricotta; and the shrimp scampi slice is so special, they only sell it on Fridays. Phantom prefers the hot chicken pizza: a fiery mix of poultry, peppers, and potatoes.

Ice Cream

GREAT ATE

THE GREATEST: Farm-Fresh Ice Cream

Richardson's Ice Cream $
156 South Main St. (Rte. 114), Middleton, MA, (978) 774-5450
www.richardsonsicecream.com

At Richardson's, the secret to the super-premium ice cream is in the freshness of the milk and cream, which come straight from the cows out back. Smooth, scrumptious flavors range from caramel flan to chocolate cheesecake. Customers lick their cones while visiting the sheep, ducks, and 300 cows on the farm, or while enjoying the batting cages, miniature golf, and heated driving range. Richardson's is also at Jordan's Furniture in Reading and at discerning ice cream counters across New England.

THE GREATEST: Bowling and Ice Cream

Ron's Gourmet Ice Cream and Bowling $
1231 Hyde Park Ave., Hyde Park, MA, (617) 364-5274

Ron's Gourmet Ice Cream and Bowling is one of the few places where bowlers can recover from a 7-10 split with a banana split. This most unusual marriage of freezer treats and candlepin makes for a family-friendly outing. The snack bar serves sumptuous ice cream creations with top-quality ingredients. Freshly baked brownies are mixed into the famous Brownie Nut ice cream, while the Coffee Madness flavor is jammed with bits of Oreo, chocolate chips, and almonds. Peanut Sunrise is made with real peanut butter swirled into a vanilla base.

THE GREATEST: Mix-Ins

Cold Stone Creamery $
9 Locations in Massachusetts
www.coldstonecreamery.com

At Cold Stone Creamery, customers choose their flavor and mix-ins and look on as the staff smooshes it all together on a slab of frozen granite. Their premium ice cream is made fresh every day, along with chocolaty brownies and crunchy waffle cones. They offer a dozen smooth, creamy ice creams, plus 40 mix-ins like Kit Kat, Snickers, Heath Bar, and Butterfinger. Or, opt for a Cold Stone original like the Birthday Cake Remix made with cake-batter ice cream, brownies, rainbow sprinkles, and gooey fudge. Locations include Boston's Theater District and the Landmark Center.

THE GREATEST: Ice Cream Playground

Kimball Farm $
400 Littleton Rd., Westford, MA, (978) 486-3891
www.kimballfarm.com

Families flock to Kimball Farm for outstanding ice cream and an entire day of entertainment. Their massive property includes a driving range, a country store, and live farm animals. There's also mini golf with full-sized working waterfalls and a 6,000-square-foot bumper boat pond. Ice cream lovers line up at the barn windows and choose from 40 intriguing flavors like Gingersnap Molasses, Grapenut, Kahlua crunch, and Butterscotch. Get your scoop on at Kimball's locations in Carlisle, Massachusetts; Saco, Maine; and Jaffrey, New Hampshire.

THE GREATEST: Exotic Flavors

Christina's Ice Cream $
1255 Cambridge St., Cambridge, MA, (617) 492-7021
www.christinasicecream.com

Christina's caters to the adventurous, sophisticated ice cream palate with more than 40 inventive flavors, inspired by their sister spice shop next door. Basics like Mexican Chocolate and Garden Fresh Mint are utterly amazing, but the awe-inspiring list continues with exotic Cardamom, Japanese Adzuki Bean, Lemon Thyme, Burnt Sugar, White Chocolate Lavender, Saffron, and Carrot Cake. Sorbets step into uncharted territory like Lemon Hibiscus or Champagne. The charming décor includes antique church pews and local art. Christina's also concocts exclusive flavors for area restaurants, like Goat Cheese ice cream for Hamersley's Bistro and Black Sesame for Ginza.

THE GREATEST: Oversized Scoops

Hodgie's $
71 Haverhill Rd., Amesbury, MA, (978) 388-1211
www.hodgies.com

When it comes to humungous helpings, Hodgie's knows how to pile on the monstrous scoops. With icy cool options like fresh fruit frappes, hot fudge and butterscotch sundaes, and fresh strawberry shortcake, the absurd portions are equally outrageous. Helpful local students shuffle steadily behind the counter, and picnic tables in a woodsy area out back allow for lingering while you lick. In addition to ice cream, Hodgie's serves hot dogs, hamburgers, and sandwiches.

THE GREATEST: Ice Cream for Ice Cream Snobs

PICCO $$

513 Tremont St., Boston, MA, (617) 929-0066

PICCO (Pizza & Ice Cream COmpany) churns out handmade ice cream in small batches with gourmet ingredients. Exquisite flavors include Scharffen Berger chocolate, Kona coffee, and Madagascar vanilla bean. Sundaes sink into classic parfait dishes with extra-tall spoons and just-whipped cream. You can even order an old-fashioned float from the soda fountain. The kitchen also slices up scrumptious pizzas finessed with toppings like bacon, onion, sour cream, and Gruyère. The retro décor looks like it's straight out of the movies, with an ice cream parlor atmosphere and cherry-colored chairs.

THE GREATEST: Italian Ice

Richie's Slush $

2084 Revere Beach Pkwy., Everett, MA, (617) 389-6407
www.richiesslush.com

Richie's Slush, a tiny take-out shack with a candy-striped roof, is one of the best ways to beat the heat. Customers queue up for slush in 18 colorful flavors like watermelon, sour blue razz, piña colada, bubble gum, almond, grape, and lemon. They also sell 28 kinds of ice cream that can be whipped into indulgent treats like brownie sundaes. Richie's sells Cool Dogs, too: clever hot dog–shaped desserts. Made by funneling vanilla soft serve into a sponge cake bun, they're topped with hot fudge, whipped cream, and jimmies.

GREAT ATE

THE GREATEST: Veal Selection

Carlo's Cucina Italiana $$
131 Brighton Ave., Allston, MA, (617) 254-9759
www.carloscucinaitaliana.com
At Carlo's Cucina Italiana, white meat is the strong suit. The never-ending menu lists red sauce classics served with a choice of chicken or veal. Dishes like jumbo shrimp in sweet Grand Marnier sauce are served in heaping helpings that are perfect for sharing. House specialties include stuffed eggplant, fusilli with sausage and broccoli rabe, and veal cutlets rolled with prosciutto, spinach, and fontina cheese. The minimalist décor keeps it casual and elbow-to-elbow seating makes it easy to sneak bites off your date's plate.

THE GREATEST: Italian Sandwich

Tutto Italiano $$
1893 River St., Hyde Park, MA, (617) 361-4700
Tutto Italiano is an authentic Italian delicatessen selling pasta, fragrant olive oils, sun-dried tomatoes, and every Italian pantry item you can imagine. Customers head to this "salute of the Boot" for wine tastings on Saturdays and custom-made sandwiches. While there's no set menu, any cold cut combination with freshly baked bread is available on request. Classic toppings include oil, vinegar, oregano, hot peppers, tomato, and basil, and they even make the mozzarella in-house. Tutto Italiano has additional locations in Wellesley, Lakeville, Hingham, and Boston's North End.

THE GREATEST: Fusilli Pasta

Bambino's $$
7 Highland Ave., Malden, MA, (781) 322-9160
www.bambinosrestaurante.com
Bambino's is a Phantom favorite for red sauce pasta like thick Fusilli Verdi sautéed with eggplant and spinach in cheesy marinara. Their signature is the hearty Tuscan Salad with garlic-roasted potatoes and Italian meats and cheeses mixed with crisp romaine lettuce, peppers, and balsamic vinaigrette. Phantom's other favorites include the Seafood Fiesta in marinara; shrimp scampi pizza with

lots of garlic; and Chicken Campagna tossed with sweet sausage, linguini, and marsala wine sauce. The Grape Room is a converted bank vault, and it's available for private dining.

THE GREATEST: Back-Door Italian

Vinny's at Night $$
76 Broadway, Somerville, MA, (617) 628-1921

Hidden in back of a convenience store (Vinny's Superette), Vinny's at Night is an unadvertised, genuine Italian eatery. The curtained-off space is cozy, with mismatched Tiffany lamps and more Italian American customers than you could shake a meatball at. Red sauce and seafood favorites team up on the Sicilian menu. The Grand Marnier shrimp are lick-the-plate delicious, as are the double-thick pork chops with sweet peppers. Expect a complimentary plate of fruit and a joke from the owner, both of which contribute to the homey feel of this unique spot.

THE GREATEST: Pasta Portions

Tomasso Trattoria & Enoteca $$
54 Turnpike Rd./Rte. 9, Southborough, MA, (508) 481-8484
www.tomassotrattoria.com

Most Italian restaurants in America serve gigantic mounds of starchy pasta, but Tomasso plates homemade noodles the traditional way: as a manageable second course before the entrée. This way you can order more plates without erupting like Mount Vesuvius. Phantom's pick is the orechietti with sausage and broccoli rabe. Tomasso is known for small antipasti plates like chickpea fries and meatballs made with ricotta cheese. And, because of the smart sizes, you'll still have room for dolci like free-form tiramisu and homemade sorbet. All of the above is served in a stylish space with a huge bar and counter seats beside the open kitchen.

THE GREATEST: Italian Mess

Comella's $$
1302 Washington St., West Newton, MA, (617) 928-1001
www.comellasrestaurant.com

Comella's is a cozy 10-seat eatery with a secret family recipe for the biggest, tastiest pasta dish Phantom has ever eaten. The Mess is an ever-changing dish, but it always contains pastas, sauce, and cheese. In fact, there's a whole menu of Messes named after the Comella family and friends. Ma's Mess is the original, and Pa's Mess is the same base with meatballs mixed in. Bear's Mess is topped with shrimp and eggplant, and Red's Mess cooks up with chicken, meatballs, and sausage. The ultimate Mess is Uncle Butch's Bomb amplified with extra everything: shells, lasagna, eggplant, chicken, veal, shrimp, meatballs, sausage, and vegetables. Comella's is super cheap and completely satisfying.

THE GREATEST: Affordable Italian American

Tre Monte $$
397 Main St., Woburn, MA, (781) 938-4020
www.tremonte.net

Just a short drive from Boston, Tre Monte offers easy parking, affordable prices, and delicious Italian American dishes. Stuffed red peppers fill out with spinach, cannellini beans, and gooey cheese; and homemade tagliatelle pasta is a hearty, buttery classic buried in Bolognese meat sauce. Phantom loves the grilled twin pork chops cut extra-thick and drizzled with rosemary tomato jus, and he always orders the impossibly light tiramisu as the grand finale.

THE GREATEST: Modern Italian

Stella $$$
1525 Washington St., Boston, MA, (617) 247-7747
www.bostonstella.com

Stella keeps the pretty, stylish people pouring through the door with a daring all-white décor combined with fine Italian dining. The crispy deep-fried arancini rice balls hide gooey pockets of buffalo mozzarella. The spicy cioppino stew, unveiled in a copper bowl, brims with tender seafood in an orange saffron broth. And Stella's Tuscan fries are topped with Parmesan and hot piquillo peppers. Late-night dining rolls until 1:30 a.m. and the modern street-side bar serves martinis until 2 a.m.

Late-Night
GREAT ATE

THE GREATEST: Late-Night Tapas

Toro $$
1704 Washington St., Boston, MA, (617) 536-4300
Open until 1 a.m., Toro has tight quarters, communal tables, and the most authentic tapas in town. Small bites include cod fritters with fried lemon, hot salted chilies, and butter grilled corn smothered in cheese. Paella contains a beautiful mix of shrimp, clams, mussels, chorizo, and chicken; and a Spanish version of sliders comes with pickled onions. The best dessert is churros with liquid chocolate for dipping. With all the drink-friendly food, Toro comes through with an all-Spanish wine list featuring sparkling cava by the pitcher, plus white and red sangria.

THE GREATEST: Cocktail Cuisine

Pho Republique $$
1415 Washington St., Boston, MA, (617) 262-0005
www.phorepublique.net
Pho Republique is a happening South End spot serving Asian fusion to a stylish crowd. This sultry after-dark eatery is set with sexy red walls and features bamboo chairs and rainbow lanterns. The kitchen keeps kicking until 1 a.m., turning out Chinatown Nachos of roasted duck and sake guacamole over wonton chips. Dim sum pupu platters might include crab dumplings or pork and ginger pot stickers. And they're known for pho, the famous Vietnamese noodle soup. Some customers come just for the fun, fruity cocktails like coconut martinis and gigantic scorpion bowls.

THE GREATEST: 24-7 Bakery

Bova's Bakery $
134 Salem St., Boston, MA, (617) 523-5601
www.northendboston.com/bovabakery
Open 24 hours, 7 days a week, Bova overflows with everything you'd want from an Italian bakery: ricotta cannoli, tiramisu, Neapolitans, cream puffs, whoopie pies, and "lobster tail" pastries. They also make oversized subs stuffed with prosciutto, buffalo mozzarella, and whole basil leaves. Calzones are baked daily, along with Sicilian pizza sold by the slice. Takeout only.

THE GREATEST: **Full Menu Into the Morning**

Franklin Café $$
278 Shawmut Ave., Boston, MA, (617) 350-0010
www.franklincafe.com

Franklin Café is a cozy martini lounge where stylish late-nighters order from a full menu until 1:30 a.m. This is where Boston's off-the-clock chefs dine and unwind. The cranberry-colored room is just big enough for nine tables, and no reservations are taken. But the wait flies by at the bar, where trendy drinks include the pear-infused Franklin sidecar. Designer comfort food includes turkey meatloaf with fig gravy and seared scallops with a puree of coconut curry cauliflower.

THE GREATEST: **Round-the-Clock Diner**

South Street Diner $
178 Kneeland St., Boston, MA, (617) 350-0028
www.southstreetdiner.com

Providing Boston with an any-hour greasy spoon, South Street Diner feeds an eclectic crowd, from celebrities to college kids, served by a motley crew of pierced and tattooed waitresses. The 1950s Worcester dining car is decked out in neon lights and vintage photos of James Dean. There's a classic jukebox and a drink list that includes beer, coffee, and chocolate frappes. The blue plate specials are dirt-cheap, ranging from cheeseburgers to banana French toast. There's also a solid selection of pie and, in warm weather, a few raised tables out on the sidewalk.

THE GREATEST: **Indian-Style Tapas**

Diva Lounge $$
248 Elm St., Somerville, MA, (617) 629-4963

Open until 1 a.m., Diva Lounge is a late-night hot spot where you can come in sneakers or stilettos. Opened by the next-door Indian eatery of the same name, this swank be-seen lounge may have Somerville's only bouncer. The unusually cool interior design includes LED lights, mirrors, and curved seating. White 3-D walls make you feel enveloped in bubble wrap. Small plates include tandoori chicken satay with sweet chili sauce, mustard lamb chops, and crab cakes served with date chutney.

THE GREATEST: Dining and Dancing

dbar $$
1236 Dorchester Ave., Dorchester, MA, (617) 265-4490
www.dbarboston.com

When you're in the mood for dinner and dancing, dbar offers the best of both worlds. After 10 p.m., the bouncers clear out the tables so customers can shake a leg right in the dining room. The fancy food is incredible, and much less expensive than the competition. The Diablo Double for two includes grilled ciabatta and olive tapenade, warm Asiago artichoke dip, greens, and crackers. Butter-melted leeks sink into the halibut entrée with clams and smoked corn. And the Angus sirloin burger is 10-ounces strong with a black pepper crust, blue cheese, and hand-cut fries.

THE GREATEST: After-Dark Delivery

News $$
150 Kneeland St., Boston, MA, (617) 426-NEWS
www.newsboston.com

News has the best late-night delivery in Boston, with door-to-door service until 5 a.m. The restaurant itself features free valet parking, shuttle service, Wi-Fi access, and newspapers lining the front hall. Every Wednesday is Ladies Night, offering a complimentary three-course dinner for females from 5 to 11 p.m. The front half is a lounge complete with leather couches, while the back revolves around the bar. Both ends offer eclectic bar food like nachos, artichoke dip, and sandwiches, plus breakfast all day and fruit smoothies.

Lobster
GREAT ATE

THE GREATEST: **Lobster Pie**

Maine Diner $
Rte. 1, Wells, ME, (207) 646-4441
www.mainediner.com

The Maine Diner sticks to tradition with huge plates of soulful Yankee fare. Their lobster pie is the best Phantom has ever had, packed with an awful lot of claw and tail meat under a buttery cracker crumb topping. Unlike other diners, they put a modern twist on their blue plate specials. The lobster Benedict and lobster club sandwich are perfect examples. The Phantom Platter is an entire meal of the Caped Critic's favorites: seafood chowder, an eight-ounce sirloin steak, baked shrimp, baked scallops, and homemade onion rings. This has to be one of the only diners in the country that grows its own herbs and vegetables out back.

THE GREATEST: **Pan-Roasted Lobster**

Jasper White's Summer Shack $$
149 Alewife Brook Pkwy., Cambridge, MA, (617) 520-9500
www.summershackrestaurant.com

Jasper White's Summer Shack is a casual clam shack with Phantom's favorite pan-roasted lobster. Cooked in bourbon and doused in melted butter with chervil and chives, it's the most decadent dish in any season! The sweet shellfish is served many different ways: wood grilled, baked and stuffed with shrimp, and wok seared with scallions and ginger. Of course, there's a classic lobster roll. The huge industrial kitchen can feed all 300 seats thanks to a 1,200-gallon lobster tank. There's a smaller Shack in Boston's Back Bay, a speedy Shack at Logan Airport, and a super Shack at Mohegan Sun.

THE GREATEST: **Lobster, Plain and Simple**

Roy Moore Lobster Co. $$
39 Bearskin Neck, Rockport, MA, (978) 546-6696

Roy Moore Lobster Co. is Phantom's favorite place for wallet-friendly lobster served simply. Not technically a restaurant, this seafood market boils lobsters on request, using ocean water to seal in a naturally briny flavor. Customers can sit out back on lobster traps while cracking open the claws. For those leaving town, Roy Moore will package live lobsters with seaweed and gel ice in an airplane-safe carton that keeps them fresh for 30 hours.

THE GREATEST: Boiled Lobster

Ogunquit Lobster Pound $$
Rte. 1, Ogunquit, ME, (207) 646-2516

Ogunquit Lobster Pound has a 20-year following for the best boiled lobster on the planet. Their secret procedure involves boiling the speckled crustaceans outside in a big pot of seawater. So many are prepared at once that the lobsters actually cook in their own juices, producing an unusual intensity of flavor. The Lobster Pound also cuts and cracks the clawed kings for you, making the succulent meal a snap to eat without the sticky, briny mess. Phantom likes to finish with any of their fresh fruit pies.

THE GREATEST: Diablo Lobster

Naked Fish $$
5 Massachusetts locations
www.nakedfish.com

Naked Fish takes two approaches to cooking seafood: "naked," which means olive oil and lemon juice, and "dressed," or smothered in flavorful sauce. Phantom won't lie . . . he loves the latter, particularly the Diablo Lobster. Pan-roasted with mussels, it comes submerged in spicy tomato basil sauce. The jumbo shrimp arrive simmering in garlic and herbs. Cuban cocktails pair perfectly, like the fresh mint mojito and the pineapple-rum Latin Love. Taken in with the samba tunes, Naked Fish is a great way to shake up the daily routine. Locations include Billerica, Framingham, Lynnfield, Waltham, and Westboro.

THE GREATEST: Baked Stuffed Lobster

Finz $$
76 Wharf St., Salem, MA, (978) 744-8485
www.hipfinz.com

Finz is parked right on the water, so you can practically spot the fresh catch of the day before it hits your plate. The lobster mac and cheese is creamy, cheesy, and decadent. The lobster roll is equally luxurious served on a buttery croissant, and the lobster ravioli are tossed with more claw meat and rich sherried cream sauce. Finz makes a mean baked, stuffed lobster bursting with luxurious stuffing made from crab, scallops, and shrimp. If you're hungry for more, check out their crispy Buffalo calamari and a second location in Dedham.

THE GREATEST: Lobster with a View

Two Lights Lobster Shack $$
225 Two Lights Rd., Cape Elizabeth, ME, (207) 799-1677
www.lobstershack-twolights.com

Located across from the historic lighthouse in Cape Elizabeth, Two Lights Lobster
Shack boasts a legendary view that's as easy to digest as the humongous lobster
dinners. From cherry-red picnic tables sprawled across the pebbled cliff, customers
dig into clam cakes and fried clams while watching the local lobstermen on the wa-
ter. Meals are ordered in the rustic seafood shack, where you can also score an
unadulterated lobster roll. While the classic is often overdone with mayo, Two
Lights serves theirs naked on a buttery grilled bun with just a dollop of the creamy
condiment on top, so you can mix it to taste. Blueberry squares and whoopie pies
round out the offerings.

THE GREATEST: Shore Dinner

Oarweed $$
65 Oarweed Rd., Ogunquit, ME, (207) 646-4022
www.oarweed.com

Oarweed is famous for two things: fresh boiled lobster and an unrivaled view of
the ocean through wall-to-wall picture windows. Combine these two, and you have
best shore dinner in all of New England. Oarweed's nautical-themed dining room
is perched above the rocky Maine coast, with crashing waves below. Steamed
clams and seafood chowder are as classic as can be, and there's a baked stuffed potato with crackly skin and a cheesy topping. Wild Maine blueberry pie is the perfect
way to finish before you head to the wash bucket sink *inside* the dining room.

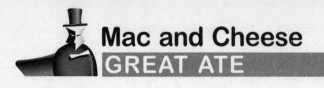

Mac and Cheese
GREAT ATE

THE GREATEST: Creamy Casserole Version

The Publick House $
1648 Beacon St., Brookline, MA, (617) 277-2880
www.thepublickhousebrookline.com
The Publick House is a cozy, curtained-off beer bar with dense, delicious mac and cheese. Their creamy casserole blends an impossible amount of Swiss, cheddar, smoked mozzarella, and Asiago with ear-shaped pasta and a discerning dose of cream. Upgrade by adding andouille sausage. The Publick's other main draw is an insanely long beer list including 27 selective draughts and 80 uncommon micro-brews by the bottle. Many of the porters and pilsners are cooked into the sophisti-cated pub grub, with results like the juicy Old Rasputin skirt steak. The Whale's Tale Pale Ale battered shrimp is crispy crunchy, and it comes with beer-infused cocktail sauce.

THE GREATEST: Gourmet Mac and Cheese

The Loft Steak and Chop House $$
1140 Osgood St. (Rte. 125), North Andover, MA, (978) 686-0026
www.loftsteakandchophouse.com
Located in a 160-year-old wooden barn, the Loft Steak and Chop House specializes in classy comfort foods like lobster mac and cheese. Melding Phantom's two fa-vorite foods into one rich dish, it features a four-cheese blend made with rotini pasta and big chunks of fresh seafood, baked until the top turns golden brown. The kitchen also turns out high-class entrées like the Celebrity Sirloin and baby back ribs. Exposed posts and beams and an inviting atmosphere epitomize the New En-gland tavern.

THE GREATEST: Just Like Mom's

Stephanie's On Newbury $$
190 Newbury St., Boston, MA, (617) 236-0990
www.stephaniesonnewbury.com
Stephanie's On Newbury is a delicious oasis after a long day of shopping. Sink into the cozy couch by the fireplace, and then sink your teeth into a crock of macaroni and cheese. The classic version is baked with three kinds of cheese and topped with

buttery breadcrumbs that brown in golden patches. Other sophisticated comfort food includes free-form, all-beef meatloaf made with cheddar cheese, and a gingerbread sundae topped with hot fudge, caramel, and molasses ice cream. When the weather heats up, there's no better people-watching than from Stephanie's sidewalk seating.

THE GREATEST: Variety

Zon's $$

2 Perkins St., Jamaica Plain, MA, (617) 524-9667
www.zonsjp.com

Zon's is a sexy, deep red dining room with funky candelabras and an updated version of old-fashioned comfort. Their mac and cheese is an over-the-top, *fromage*-filled entrée that comes in three gooey versions. The basic recipe mixes bowtie shaped farfalle pasta with a luxurious blend of sharp farmhouse cheddar and creamy, nutty fontina. There's also the Mac Daddy with garlicky chorizo sausage, and the Mac & Cheese & Peas. Zon's makes amazing burgers topped with blue cheese, caramelized onions, and bacon, and their house-fried potato chips are unbelievably addictive served with a roasted garlic dip.

THE GREATEST: Fine Dining Macaroni

Avila $$$

1 Charles St. South, Boston, MA, (617) 267-4810
www.avilarestaurant.com

Avila is a hit from the boat-shaped bar to the fine dining side. You might not expect macaroni from an elegant exhibition kitchen specializing in Mediterranean fare, but theirs is the most decadent version around. Lobster meat, blue cheese, *and* goat cheese come into the mix to create one rich dish. Avila goes all out on presentation for the flambéed halloumi cheese, served flaming with dates and cashews. There's also traditional lamb souvlaki and a rolling dessert cart. The 12-minute molten chocolate cake pairs with espresso ice cream. And the Spanish churros are like crusty cinnamon donuts, served with liquid chocolate for dipping and dunking.

THE GREATEST: Truffle Mac and Cheese

Ivy Restaurant $$

49 Temple Place, Boston, MA, (617) 451-1416
www.ivyrestaurantgroup.com

Ivy Restaurant is everything you'd expect in a new hot spot, except for high prices or uptight attitude. The menu features small plates of Italian comfort food at surprisingly low prices. Phantom's favorite is the black truffle macaroni and cheese. It gets even richer with Gorgonzola, and the whole thing is cut into a massive brick. Other favorites include seared scallops with pancetta bacon and arancini rice balls stuffed with prosciutto. The wine is unbelievably affordable, with every single bottle costing $26. The uniform pricing encourages customers to make their decision based on taste instead of price.

THE GREATEST: Classic Mac

Gibbet Hill Grill $$$
61 Lowell Rd., Groton, MA, (978) 448-2900
www.gibbethillgrill.com

Gibbet Hill Grill is set on 300 farmyard acres in a century-old barn. Both the double-sided stone fireplace and the country cuisine will warm you to the core. Aged Black Angus steaks are the specialty of the house, and they pair perfectly with classic mac and cheese. Their creamy casserole is baked with three cheeses and a butter crumb crust. Also on the stick-to-your-ribs side, the hearty shepherd's pie is capped with creamy mashed potatoes. Phantom loves the mini grilled cheese appetizer served with tomato soup for dipping. Private parties can dine in the silo room, and wedding receptions are thrown in the adjacent barn. Everyone is invited to roam the surrounding trails and apple orchard.

THE GREATEST: Fried Mac and Cheese

TGI Friday's $$
530 locations, (800) FRIDAYS
www.tgifridays.com

TGI Friday's is Phantom's favorite chain for finger foods, and their mac and cheese bites are no exception to this golden fried rule. With seven to an order, these two-bite nuggets contain elbow noodles and so much gooey cheese they practically explode through the breaded crust. They're warm and soft and great with ranch dressing for dipping. Friday's other standout starters include loaded potato skins and chicken pot stickers with sweet, tangy dipping sauce. The Tuscan spinach dip is thick and creamy, and the Wicked Wings come in unique flavors like spicy Kung Pow.

Mexican
GREAT ATE

THE GREATEST: Flan

Tu Y Yo $$
858 Broadway, Somerville, MA, (617) 623-5411
www.tuyyomexicanfonda.com
Tu Y Yo near Tufts University is as authentic as it gets. Which is why you won't
find chips, burritos, and (especially) nachos. The menu is filled with family recipes
spanning 100 years, like stuffed jalapeños, sopes, flautas, and tamales. The bisteces
en salsa "Barracha" is a house specialty made from simmering sirloin strips in a
beer-based sauce with pasilla peppers and cactus paddles. They also make Phan-
tom's favorite flan, prepared "a la Doris" with tangy cinnamon cream.

THE GREATEST: Mexican Mole

Sol Azteca $$
914 Beacon St., Boston, MA, (617) 262-0909
www.solaztecarestaurants.com
Stowed away below a sidewalk patio, Sol Azteca opens to an attractive cantina of
exposed brick, ceramic tiles, and enough Mexican collectibles to make it festive but
not fanatical. Customers can count on fruity sangria and the best mole sauce in the
whole darn city. Keeping with authentic tradition, Sol Azteca's version is a rich,
complex paste of dozens of spices, seeds, nuts, and even Mexican chocolate. The
kitchen serves it over boneless chicken breasts or cheesy enchiladas. Other old-
world dishes include grilled shrimp in garlic cilantro sauce and pork tenderloin carnitas in a chipotle orange sauce. The second location in Newton Center is even
better for outdoor dining.

THE GREATEST: Mexican Side Dishes

El Pelon $
92 Peterborough St., Boston, MA, (617) 262-9090
www.elpelon.com
El Pelon is a cramped, super-cheap eatery decorated with miniature Mexican dolls
and picnic table seating. Most recipes reflect northern Mexico's style of cooking.
While the majority of the food isn't spicy, seven hot sauces and salsas give heat
seekers plenty of options. Belly-busting burritos are offered with a choice of steak,

chicken, or pork; and the tortilla comes completely stuffed with rice, beans, cheese, lettuce, and fire-roasted salsa. The grilled chicken enchiladas are even better with sassy sides like golden fried plantains, pickled cabbage, or limed onions. If you need to cool off from all the hot peppers, the homemade horchata beverage tastes like liquid rice pudding.

THE GREATEST: Guacamole Mixed Tableside

Zocalo Cocina Mexicana $$
1414 Commonwealth Ave. Brighton, MA, (617) 277-5700
www.zocalobrighton.com
Zocalo Cocina Mexicana has the same festive energy as its sister location in Arlington, and both make the most amazing guacamole. Whipped up tableside, the creamy appetizer is mashed up in a lava rock mortar with sea salt, onion, tomato, lime, jalapeños, and even their seeds if you can stand the heat. The Mexican menu draws from Oaxaca and Veracruz, resulting in burritos, enchiladas, and Mexican pizza. They also have eight kinds of fruity, refreshing sangria in flavors like mango and peach. Phantom loves the Mexican fondue studded with spicy sausage. The cheesy chicken tacos are delicious, and the stuffed poblano peppers are batter fried and bursting with tender braised pork.

THE GREATEST: Mexican Takeout

¡Andale! $
125 Summer St., Boston, MA, (617) 737-2820
www.andaleboston.com/menu.htm
¡Andale! is a busy take-out eatery cranking out real Mexican food like chicken mole made from 27 spices. Phantom also likes the charbroiled beef with peppers and onions, the meaty portobello enchiladas, and the shredded chicken burrito that incorporates orange, tomatoes, and chile sauce. Open Monday through Friday for lunch only, the small eight-seat space is surprisingly big on atmosphere. Clay-colored walls, Mexican artifacts, and rhythmic Latin music all add up to a take-out shop you won't want to leave.

THE GREATEST: Sangria

Casa Romero $$
30 Gloucester St., Boston, MA, (617) 536-4341
www.casaromero.com
Casa Romero is a hidden gold mine of romantic atmosphere, traditional Mexican cooking, and cool margaritas. Accessible by an alleyway entrance, it's decorated in tin lamps and imported ceramic tiles from Puebla. There's also a secluded outdoor

patio for warm summer nights. Casa Romero's sangria is a sparkling beverage made from red wine steeped in brandy and fresh fruit like lemons, peaches, and apples. On the menu, house specialties include lemony posole stew and pork tenderloin with oranges and smoked chipotle peppers.

THE GREATEST: Salsa Selection

Picante Mexican Grill $
735 Massachusetts Ave., Cambridge, MA, (617) 576-6394
www.picantemex.com
Picante Mexican Grill is a tiny taqueria with Boston's best salsa selection. Customers stock up at the condiment bar on a half-dozen red and green salsas that range in heat, smokiness, and spice. There's Yankee salsa with roasted tomatoes, smoky chipotle salsa, avocado salsa, mango salsa, super-hot picante salsa, and fresh grilled jalapeño peppers. Daily specials keep the selections unpredictable, and extra touches like grilling the burritos add additional flavor and texture. Picante prides itself on using secret spice blends instead of lard, and they offer offbeat treats like portobello tacos and breakfast burritos.

THE GREATEST: Tortas

Taqueria Mexico $
24 Charles St., Waltham, MA, (781) 647-0166
The family-run Taqueria Mexico is a modest Waltham storefront, but they turn out the most amazing Mexican sandwiches. Known as tortas, these cushy sweet rolls are packed with grilled meat or seafood and finished off with creamy guacamole. The al pastor torta is piled with juicy marinated pork, while the carne asada torta has an even heftier filling of grilled steak. A dirt-cheap meal kicks off with chips and salsa or an upgrade of mountainous nachos piled high with cheese, refried beans, lettuce, tomato, onion, and jalapeños. Other menu highlights include chicken enchiladas, flautas, and chorizo burritos. Blended fruit drinks round out the offerings, and Mexican music is always streaming from the jukebox.

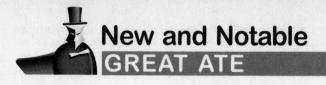

New and Notable
GREAT ATE

THE GREATEST: Comfort Food Takeout

Potbellies Kitchen $
87 A St., South Boston, MA, (617) 269-2233

For the hot, toasty sandwiches, the mouth-watering steaks, and the juicy cheese-burgers, it's easy to understand where the name came from. Specializing in comfort food, Potbellies serves quick lunches by day and affordable entrées by night. The blackboard menu lists nostalgic favorites like grilled cheese, sausage and peppers, and red sauce classics like spaghetti Bolognese. But you can also score fancier fare like pan-seared salmon and a Caesar salad with real Parmesan. There are only a handful of seats, but they turn over quickly thanks to the speedy kitchen.

THE GREATEST: Italian in the 'Burbs

Alta Strada $$
92 Central St., Wellesley, MA, (781) 237-6100
www.altastradarestaurant.com

From the mastermind behind Via Matta, Great Bay, and Radius comes Michael Schlow's next best Boston restaurant . . . in the suburbs of Wellesley. Alta Strada is a worthy reverse commute, but don't expect the same vibe as its fancy sister estab-lishments. This truly relaxing, truly affordable, truly Italian trattoria features un-fussy dishes like potato gnocchi with hot sausage and crispy roast chicken with grilled onions. For a nice, light bite, try the tomato basil pizza or an antipasto plate like sliced prosciutto with fig jam. A convenient take-out market is annexed to the 100-seat eatery.

THE GREATEST: Fresh Flavor

51 Lincoln $$
51 Lincoln St., Newton Highlands, MA, (617) 965-3100
www.51lincolnnewton.com

Crispy polenta fries, Limoncello scallops, pan-seared watermelon steak . . . creativity puts 51 Lincoln on the New and Notable map. The chef whistles his own tune with never-tasted-before flavors like skirt steak with apple-garlic jam. You might find shrimp and grits or surprising plates of "lobster noodles" with lobster roe infused in the pasta. For all the experimentation, 51 remains reliable with smooth service and a lovely dining room where the chef's own paintings evoke an art gallery. Finish with familiar desserts like Key lime pie reinvented with coconut chips and caramel cream.

THE GREATEST: Italian Splurge

Sasso $$$
116 Huntington Ave., Boston, MA, (617) 247-2400
www.sassoboston.com

Taking cues on stylish atmosphere and an Italian menu from its North End sister, Lucca, Sasso still finds its own voice. The stunning space is downright dramatic with two-story windows, soaring columns, and mezzanine dining accessible by an imported marble staircase. The oohs and aahs continue onto the plate, where blood orange electrifies tender yellowfin tuna and Maine lobster enriches creamy spaghetti carbonara with pancetta bacon. Rustic Italian breads and desserts like white chocolate peanut butter mousse ensure a memorable meal from start to finish.

THE GREATEST: Modern Indian

Mela $$
578 Tremont St., Boston, MA, (617) 859-4805

Playing to its South End neighborhood, Mela is as modern as they come. The exotic soundtrack adds to the trendy atmosphere, and a stylish audience applauds the Indian cuisine, some of which is cooked on 500-degree hot stones. Copper accents, sheer curtains, and hanging balloon lamps make the space feel young and flirty. Phantom suggests starting with a mango martini before digging into lunch buffet basics like chicken tikka masala, crispy fried samosa pastries, and mild curries. More adventurous creations include mustard lamb chops. Mela's garlic naan is a good, puffy rendition of India's signature bread.

THE GREATEST: North End Newbie

La Galleria 33 $$
125 Salem St., Boston, MA, (617) 723-7233
www.lagalleria33.com

La Galleria 33 is off the beaten path in the North End, but it's worth pushing past the stellar eats on Hanover Street to get to this romantic new trattoria. The open-hearth kitchen perfects classics like chicken Parm, homemade lasagna, and linguini with clams. But they also serve incredible shrimp Parmigiana and veal paradiso stuffed with prosciutto and mozzarella. Both candlelit rooms have a warm, inviting atmosphere, and the glass doors swing open for alfresco dining.

THE GREATEST: Café and Restaurant

Z Square $$
14 JFK St., Cambridge, MA, (617) 576-0101
www.z-square.com

Bringing two new venues to the Harvard community, Z Square splits between a casual café upstairs and a stylish dining room accessible past the alfresco alley seating. The underground bistro houses a lengthy bar, round banquettes, and modern glass partitions that section off areas for private partying. Bold, global dishes span from seared tuna to seafood paella to jerk chicken with pineapple. Up at street level, the cafeteria-style snack shop is like a diner designed for urban college kids. Come early for breakfast, grab a mid-day crepe or sandwich, or unwind late night with cookies or a beer.

THE GREATEST: Upscale Burger

POPS $$
560 Tremont St., Boston, MA, (617) 695-1250
www.popsrestaurant.net

The South End is known for high-end eats and dive bar bargains, but POPS gives it a dining option that's happily in between. The stretched bar is perfect for observing the exhibition kitchen through a wall of glass. But the other walls are just as interesting, made of intricate black and white patterns and featuring flat-screen TVs displaying antique Boston photos. Modern comfort food starts with stuffed quahogs and gigantic sides like cheesy bacon pesto gnocchi. Diners can keep it casual with a shrimp po'boy or the caramelized onion burger, or they can upgrade to Asian salmon or lamb Bolognese.

Outdoor Dining
GREAT ATE

THE GREATEST: Snacks and Swimming

Roof Top Pool $$$
Colonnade Hotel, 120 Huntington Ave., Boston, MA, (617) 424-7000
www.rooftoppool.com

There's nothing quite like a frozen daiquiri while watching the sunset across the Boston skyline. Twelve stories above the city, the Roof Top Pool on the Colonnade Hotel provides a secret oasis of sun and fun. From Memorial Day to Labor Day, waiters double as lifeguards while serving cocktails and light lunches. There's a lobster-crab martini, coconut shrimp, and a tasty blue cheeseburger. Admission is free for hotel guests but the visiting public can purchase a day pass. Call for current pricing.

THE GREATEST: Island Dining

Rockmore Floating Restaurant $$
94 Wharf St., Salem, MA, (617) 740-1001
www.therockmore.com

Snuggled amongst the boats in beautiful Salem Harbor, the Rockmore is an unusual floating restaurant. It's completely surrounded by water, buoyed by a system of tanks. It's only accessible by water, so customers can motor up and tie off or take the shuttle from the mainland. The onboard kitchen and full bar are set up for seafood dishes like lobster rolls and fisherman's platters piled high with fried clams and shrimp. Landlubbers can chow down on bacon burgers and turkey roll-ups.

THE GREATEST: Harborside Seafood

Barking Crab $$
88 Sleeper St., Boston, MA, (617) 426-2722
www.barkingcrab.com

Hungry for the city's finest seafood? Head to Great Bay, Legal Sea Foods, or Neptune Oyster. But if it's waterside dining and imbibing you want, the Barking Crab is perfect. The tent-covered, open-air deck is lined with picnic tables and draws a loud, lively after-work crowd. The Fort Point Channel view of the Financial District is grand, and it's perfectly relaxed. Stick to basics like peel-and-eat shrimp and fish and chips. They do a decent job with the traditional New England clambake, and the rock on your table helps crack open the lobster.

THE GREATEST: **Backyard BBQ**

Curtis' Bar-B-Que. $

Rte. 5 (exit 4 off I-91), Putney, VT., (802) 387-5474
www.curtisbbqvt.com

Some people raise pigs to roast; others raise them as pets. At Curtis' Bar-B-Que, they do both. Customers visit C.J, the grill master's beloved pot-bellied friend and supervisor, before lining up for amazing BBQ. Most of the magic happens under a tin roof in the hardwood pit, but you'll be equally amazed at the kitchen, which operates out of a retired school bus. The menu lists chicken, ribs, and pork, which can be enjoyed at picnic tables scattered across the lawn. Phantom also recommends the pork-stuffed baked potato spilling over with sauce and hunks of white meat.

THE GREATEST: **Sidewalk Seating**

Armani Café $$$

214 Newbury St., Boston, MA, (617) 437-0909

Boston's beautiful people gravitate toward Newbury Street. If they're not eating at Armani Café, then they're sure to walk by on the way to Stephanie's or Sonsie. Armani's sidewalk seating is perfect for catching all the action, and it's especially popular with a young Euro crowd. With options like avocado salads and thin-crust pizza, it's tasty, too. Phantom's favorite is the lobster fra diavolo over linguine, followed by creamy tiramisu. Timed with the setting sun, Armani Café is just where you want to be on a beautiful summer night.

THE GREATEST: **Garden Patio**

B&G Oysters Ltd. $$$

550 Tremont St., Boston, MA, (617) 423-0550
www.bandgoysters.com

B&G is well known for fresh seafood, but it's also one of the best outdoor dining spots in Boston. The sunken stone patio off the back is like a secret garden, and it's perfect for a summer meal or a private party. B&G is the city's hottest raw bar, offering a dozen oyster varieties from a rotating list of 40. The selection is so fresh, it even changes between lunch and dinner. Customers can sit around the open kitchen and order stuffed calamari in bacon vinaigrette or a fried goat cheese salad. The lobster BLT is a lovely departure from the classic lobster roll, and sweet shrimp dumplings glisten in miso oil.

THE GREATEST: **Waterfront Dining**

Intrigue Café $$

Boston Harbor Hotel, 70 Rowes Wharf, Boston, MA, (617) 856-7744
www.bhh.com/intrigue.htm

Intrigue Café boasts premium harborside seating, with tables that spill onto the sidewalk. Tucked behind the Boston Harbor Hotel, the lounge is 20 feet from the bobbing yachts tied off at Rowes Wharf. The global kitchen keeps a "clock-free" menu, so customers can order breakfast at sundown and dinner all day. Best of all, every bargain-priced dish comes out of the same kitchen as Meritage, the fine dining restaurant upstairs. Highlights include roasted lobster with sweet corn pudding, cheddar cheeseburgers, and butternut squash sage ravioli.

THE GREATEST: **Sunken Seating**

Bouchée $$

159 Newbury St., Boston, MA, (617) 450-4343
www.boucheebrasserie.com

Bouchée is a fun social scene with killer outdoor dining. Set below street level, the spectacular patio feels more private than sidewalk seating. You'll still get plenty of sun, along with classic brasserie dishes and raw bar seafood. If you're on a date, try the two-person whole roasted truffle chicken. The smoked ham and onion flatbread is also perfect for sharing. This is the place for classics like coq au vin (chicken braised in wine) and steak frites with an upgraded cut of aged sirloin. For dessert, there's a lineup of chocolate mousse, profiteroles, sorbet, and crème brûlée.

Pizza
GREAT ATE

THE GREATEST: Cheese Pizza

Pizzeria Regina $
11 ½ Thacher St., Boston, MA, (617) 227-0765
www.pizzeriaregina.com

Pizzeria Regina is *the* North End destination for traditional Neapolitan pizza, cooked in a piping hot, century-old brick oven. A special blend of mozzarella, pecorino, and Romano cheeses results in fabulous glimmers of oil. If you want to eat like a real Italian, pour on some hot pepper oil. Phantom loves the margherita pizza with fresh basil, which Regina recommends with a well-done crust. St. Anthony's Pizza wears creamy, garlicky white sauce and hunks of sausage, and the three-pound Giambotta is so bombarded with peppers, onions, mushrooms, and pepperoni, you can barely see the crust.

THE GREATEST: Slice and Salad Combo

Upper Crust $
20 Charles St., Boston, MA, (617) 723-9600
www.theuppercrustpizzeria.com

The Upper Crust turns out fantastic thin-crust pizza in imaginative combinations. Communal dining and counter service make this pizzeria perfect for grabbing a quick slice, and the metal wave ceiling gives the space a hip industrial atmosphere. The menu focuses on Neapolitan-style pies with 30 toppings and specialty preconceived pies. Phantom digs the chicken pesto pie with garlic and Gorgonzola and the Uncommon Pizza topped with bacon, pineapple, and jalapeños. One of the best deals in Boston is their $5 combo, which includes the slice of the day and a Greek salad. Locations include Coolidge Corner, Newbury Street, Lexington, and Hingham.

THE GREATEST: Old-School Pies

Santarpio's Pizza $
111 Chelsea St., Boston, MA, (617) 567-9871

Santarpio's is a grimy pizza shop with feisty waiters who yell at anyone in their way. It's a dive bar, and that's the charm of the place. Plus, they make the most classic, old-school pies around. The crust is perfectly chewy and crisp, and traditional toppings don't stray far from pepperoni, mushrooms, and onions. Their absolute best is the garlicky white pie with sausage. The only appetizer is barbecued lamb and sausage, served piping hot with Italian bread and cherry peppers. If you can take your eyes of the pies, there's a collection of autographed boxing pictures around the ripped vinyl benches and Formica tables.

THE GREATEST: Clay-Oven Flatbread

The Flatbread Company $$
5 Market Sq., Amesbury, MA, (978) 834-9800
www.flatbreadcompany.com

The Flatbread Company's free-form pies are cooked in a massive dome-shaped clay oven that's right in the middle of the dining room. They call them flatbreads, and the crust is made from organic wheat and spring water, resulting in a slim structure you can really chew on. There's Jay's Heart made with whole milk mozzarella and wood-fired "cauldron" tomato sauce, and the Punctuated Equilibrium Pie with olives, roasted peppers, goat cheese, and rosemary. Desserts like the root beer float and the brownie and ice cream go over well with kids, who will also love the open, earthy setting. Additional Flatbread locations include Portland, Maine; Portsmouth, New Hampshire; and Bedford, Massachusetts.

THE GREATEST: White Clam Pizza

Frank Pepe Pizzeria $$
157 Wooster St., New Haven, CT, (203) 865-5762
www.pepespizzeria.com

Frank Pepe is so revered by pizza aficionados that New Yorkers hop the train out of Manhattan just to eat here. It's in the middle of New Haven's famous Little Italy, but Pepe is *the* place to get coal-fired Neapolitan pies. They're cooked in an ancient brick oven, resulting in a texture that's nice and chewy with a crispy, crackly crust. For something superlative, try their legendary white clam pie, a garlicky Parmesan platform loaded with briny seafood. The pizza chefs practically dance around the tiled open kitchen, shuffling the longest pizza peels Phantom has ever seen. Their sister shop is the Spot next door, and there's a second Frank Pepe in Fairfield.

THE GREATEST: Sicilian Pizza

Pinocchio's $
74 Winthrop St., Cambridge, MA, (617) 876-4897
www.pinocchiospizza.net

What makes Pinocchio's pizza so special is the crust. It's light and crispy, airy and addictive. All the traditional toppings are available, like pepperoni, sausage, peppers, onions, and mushrooms. The most popular slice is the tomato basil with fresh mozzarella and lots of salt and pepper. The pizza is incredibly cheap, and slices can be boxed up and out the door in a minute. Though most customers come for the pizza, there's also one heck of a steak and cheese. It's stuffed with a big slice of sirloin and smothered in peppers and onions.

THE GREATEST: Shrimp Garlic Pizza

Kelley Square Pub $
84 Bennington St., East Boston, MA, (617) 567-4627

Everybody knows Santarpio's, but around the corner is one of the most underrated pizzerias in Boston. Kelley's has the kind of friendly atmosphere you'd expect from a neighborhood watering hole, but the pizzas are way above average. The crust is well done, and puffy around the edge. You can order standard toppings like cheese, pepperoni, and hamburger, but for an extra-special slice, try the shrimp garlic pie with loads of seafood popping up out of the golden cheese mantle.

THE GREATEST: Bar Pie

Wonder Bar $
121 Shrewsbury St., Worcester, MA, (508) 752-9909

Wonder Bar is worth a drive for two reasons: seeing a guitar shaped like a slice of pizza and eating the best pepperoni pizza ever! This blue-collar watering hole serves amazing bar pies, individual servings that go great with a cold beer. The medium-thick crust sings a saucy symphony while welding together the toppings with plenty of cheese. A close second to the loaded pepperoni, the Combination Pizza triples up on peppers, mushrooms, and sausage. There's plenty of Italian American fare like chicken Parm with ziti and meatball subs, and don't forget to check out the rock star photos around the bar.

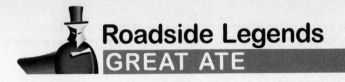

Roadside Legends
GREAT ATE

THE GREATEST: Roadside Dogs

Flo's Steamed Hot Dogs $
Rte. 1, Cape Neddick, Maine, No Phone

Flo's ranks among the best roadside wieneries in the entire country, serving delectable dogs that can be downed in three bites. Most people should aim for a minimum of four, as only a "Flo virgin" would order less. Despite the low, sloping ceiling and just six wooden stools, the sassy owner can boast of quite a lunch-counter community. There's not much to eat here except outstanding hot dogs on silky, steamed buns. Made in-house, the incredible hot sauce is a top-secret blend of BBQ sauce and caramelized onions with a spicy, salty bite that goes well with mayo. Flo's is open for lunch only, every day except Wednesday.

THE GREATEST: Affordable Family Outing

Mendon Twin Drive-In $
35 Milford St. (Rte. 16), Mendon, MA, (508) 473-5840
www.mendondrivein.com

Mendon Twin Drive-In is one of the few remaining outdoor movie theaters in New England. With two screens and a capacity of 800 vehicles, they show first-run movies every night during the summer. At $20 per carload, you can stuff as many people as possible in your car for a back-to-back, two-movie show. The sound is broadcast over AM/FM stereo, and patrons are welcome to toss Frisbees in the grassy drive-in field. The atypical snack bar is decorated in '50s memorabilia, and offers wing dings, mozzarella sticks, and popcorn chicken alongside taco dogs, nachos, and jalapeño poppers.

THE GREATEST: Lobster Hut

Bob Lobster $$
49 Plum Island Tpk. Newbury, MA, (978) 456-7100
www.boblobster.com

Few seafood shacks catch their own lobsters, but Bob Lobster is a delicious exception. They reel and deal fresh catches and then sell them super cheap. Live, steamed, or mixed into a roll or a salad . . . their lobster is the best around. They also deep-fry fresh lobster, stew a creamy lobster chowder, and offer ready-to-bake lobster pies for takeout. Picnic tables overlook the Merrimack River, and it's all down the road from the sandy beaches on Plum Island. Richardson's Ice Cream is scooped into cups and cones for dessert.

THE GREATEST: Beans and Dogs

Gilley's $
175 Fleet St., Portsmouth, NH, (603) 431-6343
www.gilleyspmlunch.com
For cheap burgers and delicious dogs from lunch to late night, Phantom heads to Gilley's. This classic Worcester diner car still has the original oak and porcelain intact, and all-American classics remain the menu staples. Kraut dogs and cheese dogs give way to chiliburgers. The beans and dogs combo compiles twin weenies atop maple-baked beans, with buttered white bread on the side. Seasoned customers know the lingo when ordering a burger. "The works" means mustard, relish, and onion. "Loaded" means "the works" plus ketchup.

THE GREATEST: Lobster Roll

The Tamarack $$
691 Endicott St. N., Laconia, NH, (603) 366-4687
The Tamarack is a Weirs Beach legend, and their all-time lobster roll record is 881 sold in a single day. Their creamy, dense version contains a hint of celery plus two kinds of meat: Maine lobster and the sweeter Chilean rock lobster. Like all the seafood rolls, it can be upgraded to a 10-inch jumbo bun. Other seafood shack classics include crunchy fried scallops, thick chocolate frappes, and oddities like frog legs and alligator piled into the Southern PuPu Basket. The onion rings come in sweet center nuggets, finger rings, and standard rings; they're so darn popular, "The Rack" employs an entire team to do nothing but fry them to order.

THE GREATEST: Midnight Munchies on Wheels

Haven Brothers Diner $
Corner of Fulton and Dorrance streets, Providence, RI 02903
(401) 861-7777
Haven Brothers in Providence is a mobile stainless steel diner on wheels. Every evening it rolls into City Hall around 5 p.m. and plugs into an electric outlet that fires up the grill until 4 a.m. Politicians and professionals stop by on their way home, followed by partygoers looking for a late-night nosh. Phantom loves the All-The-Way Dogs (mustard, onions, relish, and celery salt), bacon cheeseburgers, and chili cheese fries. The outrageously messy Murder Burger is a double-decker piled high with cheese, chili, bacon, mushrooms, onions, lettuce, tomatoes, and mayonnaise.

THE GREATEST: Grilled Onion Burger

White Hut $
280 Memorial Ave., West Springfield, MA, (413) 736-9390
www.whitehut.com
White Hut is home of the best onion burger Phantom has ever savored. It starts as an ordinary griddle patty on a soft white bun, but then it's topped with a luscious mass of fried onions. These golden strings are slowly cooked in a steaming pile on the back of the stove, where they caramelize into something so very sweet and tender. Though the open kitchen cooks may be the quickest in the state, you'll still find your hot dog bun grilled golden on the outside. Twelve floor-mounted stools line the Formica counter, and customers are on the honor system as they rattle off what they ate and cash out.

THE GREATEST: Hot Lobster Roll

Clam Shack $$
2 Western Ave. (Rte. 9), Kennebunk, Maine, (207) 967-2560
Located across the Kennebunk Bridge, the Clam Shack's menu is practically hoisted up over the bank. Customers stop by the waterside seafood shanty for fried favorites and the best hot lobster roll around. Unlike its mayonnaise-smothered cousin, this dainty version is served warm with melted butter and stuffed on a toasted bun in big hunks from a one-pound lobster. The onion rings are light and addictive, and the clam chowder comes sweet and creamy. Kids can dig into whole belly clams or a gooey grilled cheese, and the whole family can park it on a bench overlooking the water.

Romantic
GREAT ATE

THE GREATEST: Exotic Atmosphere

Tangierino $$$
83 Main St., Charlestown, MA, (617) 242-6009
www.tangierino.com

Tangierino is a lavish date place with exotic North African flavor. The Moroccan menu favors olive oil, grains, and fruit, resulting in sweet-savory dishes. Phantom can't resist their traditional tagines served in a cone-shaped clay dish. Sultan's Kadra layers tender lamb over cheesy eggplant fritters, fig candy, and rich rosemary reduction. For an exciting starter, the chicken b'stila comes as flaky phyllo stuffed with almonds and cinnamon and is served with mint yogurt. Moroccan mint tea is a sweet ending, as beautiful belly dancers make their way around the velvet seats and into the adjoining Casbah Lounge, which features hookahs.

THE GREATEST: Flirty Cocktails

Cuchi Cuchi $$
795 Main St., Cambridge, MA, (617) 864-2929
www.cuchicuchi.net

Cuchi Cuchi flaunts a stylish, eccentric eatery that'll put any couple in the mood for flirty cocktails. The talented bartenders, dressed in black with flashy rhinestones, hand-muddle concoctions like the strawberry basil martini and the blackberry Cosmo. The gorgeous old-world bar is set with ornate stained glass purchased on eBay, and the international menu is tapas-style for sharing. Phantom's favorite small dishes are the tuna, salmon, and watermelon tartar; the grilled pork rolled around pancetta bacon and garlic; and the cookie cornucopia dessert overflowing with fruit and whipped cream.

THE GREATEST: Skyline Dining

Top of the Hub $$$
Prudential Center, Boston, MA, (617) 536-1775
http://www.prudentialcenter.com/dine/topofthehub.html

The Top of the Hub greets diners on the 52nd floor of the Prudential Center, where live jazz and the Boston skyline make for a spectacular, memorable meal. The mouthwatering New American menu is as moving as the distant sunset, offering mile-high standouts like spicy lobster soup in ginger coconut broth. The thick tuna steak is encrusted with macadamia nuts. And the incredible cookie plate is baked-to-order, stacked with sugar cookies, chocolate walnut cookies, and chocolate chip cookies, plus cinnamon whipped cream and fresh berries! Surrounded by city lights and a bird's-eye view of Fenway Park, the mood is unbelievably romantic.

THE GREATEST: Rustic Fine Dining

White Barn Inn $$$
37 Beach Ave., Kennebunk, Maine, (207) 967-2321
www.whitebarninn.com
The dazzling White Barn Inn is the ultimate in rustic fine dining, blending antiques and candle lighting with crystal and sterling silver. This nineteenth-century setting features live piano music and tuxedo-dressed waiters who unveil everyone's dish with theatrical coordination. The four-course prix fixe menu features New England cuisine like steamed Maine lobster tail with ginger carrots over cognac butter fettuccine. The beef Wellington is the ultimate comfort food of juicy steak encased in pastry. Other tasty treats include blood orange sorbet and rich banana pudding with milk chocolate mousse and roasted banana ice cream.

THE GREATEST: North End Escape

Marco Cucina Romana $$
253 Hanover St., Boston, MA, (617) 742-1276
www.marcoboston.com
Making a quiet, romantic escape on the North End's main drag seems as likely as Phantom scoring a date in the first place, but this second-floor hideaway lies well above the street bustle. The home-style Italian menu includes big bowls of unfussy pasta and house-cured salumi that are as authentic Italian as it gets. Menu highlights include gnocchi with brown butter and sage, veal osso buco, and fried polenta. Most couples slink off to a candlelit corner, but singles can look for love at the stool-lined food bar alongside the open kitchen. On Sundays, the chef does a special menu served family-style.

THE GREATEST: Tableside Dinner for Two

Salts $$$
798 Main St., Cambridge, MA, (617) 876-8444
www.saltsrestaurant.com
Salts achieves a rare level of delicious dining. The place is so darn small that your date will be forced to sit within whispering distance. Servers spend extra time describing dishes in luscious detail, so your mouth will be watering before the flat

iron beef with truffle honey-glazed vegetables even touches the table. The ballotine of chicken is the most succulent slow-roasted bird Phantom has ever eaten, and the lemon soufflé tart is like eating warm citrus clouds on a sugar cookie crust. For a special treat, order the whole roasted duck for two, carved tableside and served with truffled peaches. Don't even think about going without a reservation.

THE GREATEST: Romantic French Food

Sel de la Terre $$$
255 State St., Boston, MA, (617) 720-1300
www.seldelaterre.com

Phantom can't help but fall in love at Sel de la Terre . . . at least with the Southern French food. There's nothing like seared scallops with smoked bacon and wild mushrooms to bring on a delicious, starry-eyed spell. The skillet pork chop pairs with roasted apples and pears, and the applewood-smoked chicken sizzles over lemon spaetzle and artichokes. Their signature rosemary pommes frites are the most herbaceous, awesome fries you'll ever eat. The chef is proud of his crusty breads, which are sold in the adjoining boulangerie. New locations are set for Natick and the Mandarin Oriental in the Back Bay.

THE GREATEST: Cozy Nook

Taberna de Haro $$
999 Beacon St., Brookline, MA, (617) 277-8272

Taberna de Haro serves some of the tastiest tapas this side of Madrid. A traditional brick oven infuses fragrant garlic into almost every dish. Spanish bar foods are divided into small snack-sized plates and larger casseroles, with highlights like mixed paella with the most tender shrimp, clams, calamari, chicken, and beef. All the expected dishes are present and accounted for: jamon Serrano, tortilla espanola (potato egg omelet), hot garlic shrimp, and creamy flan. But there are adventurous treats, too, like fried shark and veal sausage. Luckily for couples, the undersized tables practically force you to eat off each other's plates.

Sandwich
GREAT ATE

THE GREATEST: Fast Food Deli

Sam LaGrassa's $
44 Province St., Boston, MA, (617) 357-6861
www.samlagrassas.com
This lunch-only deli boasts "fresh from the pot" corned beef, honey-baked ham, and aged Black Angus roast beef, which are all roasted, baked, and sliced in-house. Phantom recommends the Famous Rumanian Pastrami Sandwich piled with sweet, ever-so-tender meat. Grilled sandwiches are good, too, with combos like turkey, honey-baked ham, melted Swiss, and creamy coleslaw. Suits and students cram into the communal tables and smoosh alongside the stand-up counters. But the cafeteria-style line moves quickly, and it's quite a sight to watch the monster meat-slicer going nonstop.

THE GREATEST: Chilean Sandwich

Chacarero $
426 Washington St., Boston, MA, (617) 542-0392
www.chacarero.com
Chacarero is not only the name of this tiny takeout counter in Downtown Crossing; it's also the main menu item: a cheap Chilean sandwich on plush round bread that comes hot of the grill and is bigger than you can imagine. The tasty contents include grilled chicken or beef, Muenster cheese, tomatoes, roasted red peppers, avocado, and steamed green beans. Measuring nine whopping inches across, they're also available BBQ-style with extra spice. Phantom likes to round out the meal with sweet potato fries or an enormous beef empanada. The bigger Province Street location has tables for sit-down dining.

THE GREATEST: Quirky Sandwiches

Darwin's Limited $
148 Mt. Auburn St., Cambridge, MA, (617) 354-5233
www.darwinsltd.com
Darwin's Limited resembles an authentic general store lined with an adjoining café. But they offer spectacular sandwiches. The Sparks is slicked with horseradish scallion mayo and piled high with roast beef, while the Appleton features sweet-savory

chicken salad mixed with celery, apples, and raisins. Daily specials include dishes such as grilled ham steak with melted Brie. The sandwich makers are the quickest in their league, and they can even create two at the same time. There's a second location on the other side of Harvard's campus (Cambridge Street) that offers the same free wireless Internet access.

THE GREATEST: Corned Beef

Michael's Deli   **$**
256 Harvard St., Brookline, MA, (617) 738-3354

Michael's Deli is a hole-in-the-wall sandwich king serving superior cold cuts and unbelievable corned beef. The menu may not be kosher, but Jewish deli items are imported daily from the Big Apple. They've got all the delicious basics, including warm potato knishes, dill pickles, and authentic New York–style bagels. Their gargantuan sandwiches cost next to bubkes, like the Thanksgiving Sandwich of warm turkey breast, tangy cranberry, and soft stuffing. Phantom can barely fit his mouth around the four-inch Michael's Choice Sandwich, combining prime rib, beef brisket, and horseradish sauce.

THE GREATEST: Classic Sandwiches

All Star Sandwich Bar   **$**
1245 Cambridge St., Cambridge, MA, (617) 868-3065
www.allstarsandwichbar.com

Peanut butter and jelly . . . the Reuben . . . the muffaletta. They're all classics, and they're all available at All Star Sandwich Bar. The Gobbler goes *holiday gourmet* with roast turkey, apple sausage stuffing, and orange cranberry relish, while the Monte Cristo melds ham, turkey, and melted Swiss between grilled French toast. The Beef on Weck piles warm roast beef on a crusty kimmelweck bun, served with horseradish for spreading and au jus for dipping. All Star is a fun, colorful, full-service sandwich bar, and it's just a few doors down from its sister restaurant, East Coast Grill (see the Brunch Great Ate).

THE GREATEST: Six-Foot Steak Bombs

T. C. Lando's   **$**
127 Main St., Hudson, MA, (978) 568-9432
www.thecheesesteakguys.com

Forget about Philly; the best cheesesteaks in the country come from T. C. Lando's. Their steak bombs pack more than a pound of meat made from a secret two-beef blend. They'll even turn out a six-foot sub if you special order it. Their 30 cheesesteaks include the Firecracker with pepperoni and tomato sauce; the Kama-Kazi includes sausage, ham, bacon, and BBQ sauce; and the Mis-Steak loads up on meatballs, sausage, mushrooms, and onion. Beyond beefy beasts, there are incredible calzones, burritos, and Italian pizzas. Acton is home to their second location, and the same steak bombs are found at their sister restaurants: Tory's in Leominster and Carl's Steak Subs in Waltham.

THE GREATEST: Cubano Sandwich

El Oriental de Cuba $
416 Centre St., Jamaica Plain, MA, (617) 524-6464
The legendary El Oriental de Cuba is one of the best bargains around Boston. Their Cuban sandwich is grilled until hot and crispy and overstuffed with roast pork, cured ham, pickles, Swiss cheese, and mustard. It's offered with other house specialties like eggs and chorizo, shredded beef with sauce, hearty rice and beans, and rich chicken soup. Sides like fried plantains round out the meal, and tropical shakes are made to order with exotic fruits like mango, papaya, or guanabana. El Oriental is one of those rare full-service eateries where every item is amazingly cheap and delicious.

THE GREATEST: Panini

Domenic's Italian Bakery and Deli $
987 Main St., Waltham, MA, (781) 899-3817
www.getdoms.com
Domenic's Italian Bakery and Deli sells the best panini on house-baked ciabatini rolls. Phantom's favorite is the Parma ham panini stuffed with fresh mozzarella and basil-marinated tomatoes. The Pollo panini contains breaded chicken cutlets, roasted peppers, capers, and goat cheese. The Tonno combines imported yellow tuna and black olive tapenade. Other Italian temptations include saltimbocca calzones stuffed with veal and prosciutto, cheese ravioli in marinara, homemade lasagna, Sicilian pizza by the slice, and authentic cannoli. There are few tables, but the counter system is set up for takeout.

Seafood
GREAT ATE

THE GREATEST: Seafood Market

Belle Isle Seafood $
1267 Saratoga St., East Boston, MA, (617) 567-1619
With only six seats in this tiny shack, most customers get their meal to go. Belle
Isle is where seafood lovers shop for oversized lobster rolls. Each one is packed
with a half-pound of meat, and the bargain basement price is one of the lowest
Phantom has ever seen. Other options include the baked stuffed lobster filled with
shrimp, scallops, and crab, and there's a buttery lobster pie baked with bread
crumbs. They also sell a boatload of fresh fish straight from the docks that you can
take home and cook yourself.

THE GREATEST: Seafood Chain

Legal Sea Foods $$$
14 Massachusetts locations
www.legalseafoods.com
Legal has grown from tiny market into *the* seafood authority of Boston and be-
yond. After 60 years in the business, they know where to get the freshest fish.
Their expertise shows on a menu of 40-plus seafood selections, including Phan-
tom's favorite clam chowder. There's something for everyone, from classic lump
crab cakes to innovative oven-roasted rainbow trout stuffed with cornbread and
pancetta. Fried clams and coconut shrimp make great guilty pleasures, but adven-
turous types might like the falafel salmon or the Alaskan butterfish in wasabi
cream. Locations include the Prudential Center, Long Wharf, Chestnut Hill, and
Park Square.

THE GREATEST: Seafood at Brunch

Lineage $$$
242 Harvard St., Brookline, MA, (617) 232-0065
www.lineagerestaurant.com
Lineage is on fire for seafood, with a daily changing menu. You might find seared
scallops with tender gnocchi, or soft-shell crabs with guacamole and mango salsa.
The salt cod beignets are like savory donuts that come with slab bacon and beans.
The kitchen really shines at Sunday brunch, when scrambled eggs and home fries

can't compare to buttermilk fried shrimp or crab cakes with corn salsa. Many dishes are cooked in a wood oven in the dining room, and Lineage gets special lobster deliveries from the chef's cousin, a local lobsterman.

THE GREATEST: Raw Bar

Neptune Oyster $$
63 Salem St., Boston, MA, (617) 742-3474
www.neptuneoyster.com

Every table at Neptune Oyster starts with a bowl of oyster crackers, but don't fill up before tasting the freshest raw bar around. There are at least a dozen different oysters and one amazing shellfish platter with the usual cocktail shrimp and oysters, plus littlenecks, lobster tail, and dipping sauces on the side. Giving a nod to the North End, the kitchen turns out Italian seafood like fried calamari and shellfish stew with saffron rice. They offer a superlative lobster roll two ways: cold with mayo or warm with butter. Either way, you get a pile of crispy fries.

THE GREATEST: Fisherman Recommended

No Name Restaurant $$
15 1/2 Fish Pier, Boston, MA, (617) 338-7539

No Name Restaurant isn't marked by a sign or even a name, but this nautical-themed eatery is worth the search. Traditional New England seafood is served in a rustic double-decker, and the harborside location on the Boston Fish Pier explains the freshness of the food. Their juicy fried clams taste clean and crispy, and the seafood chowder is filled with fish instead of potato fillers. Phantom loves the sautéed lobster, shrimp, and scallops in white wine butter sauce. If you stick around, the sweet reward is strawberry rhubarb pie or Grape-Nuts custard.

THE GREATEST: Italian-Style Seafood

Out of the Blue $$
215 Elm St., Somerville, MA, (617) 776-5020
www.outofthebluerestaurant.com

Out of the Blue offers Italian seafood in the heart of Davis Square. It's casual enough to bring the kids, who will love the underwater atmosphere from wall-to-wall ocean murals. The Italian-style kitchen offers skillfully prepared seafood like shrimp scampi and stuffed calamari in plum tomato sauce. Littlenecks "Italian style" are simmered in white wine broth with grilled onions, and clams and linguini are a house specialty. Phantom's favorite is the spicy Lobster Fra Diablo brimming with tender calamari and plump scallops. For dessert, don't miss the classic tiramisu.

THE GREATEST: **Seafood Paella**

Olives $$$

10 City Square, Charlestown, MA, (617) 242-1999

www.toddenglish.com

On rare occasions you can spot Todd English in the stonewall exhibition kitchen, but the real reason to reserve at Olives is the eclectic Mediterranean cuisine. Phantom's favorite is the Paella Olivacious: a deluxe seafood ensemble of shrimp, lobster, clams, mussels, chorizo, and chicken. Even better is the brick-oven baked rice dish topped with wood-grilled swordfish. They also make a mean roasted pumpkin lobster risotto and a chicken wing appetizer stuffed with sausage and glazed with hot pepper sauce. If you want to keep the feast going, indulge in the vanilla bean soufflé topped with ice cream.

THE GREATEST: **Bistro Seafood**

Eastern Standard $$$

Hotel Commonwealth, 528 Commonwealth Ave., Boston, MA,
(617) 532-9100

www.easternstandardboston.com

Eastern Standard is the closest to Paris you can get in Boston. This high-energy bistro offers heated sidewalk seating, a gorgeous 46-foot marble bar, and handsome red leather banquettes. Pristine oysters are shucked at the raw bar in the back, where you can also spot Alaskan King crab legs and shrimp cocktail. Eastern Standard is one of the few places you can order an appetizer that includes a side of fries. Their mussels and frites is a double pleasure, and the seafood is braised in Vermont cider for sweet flavor. Other attractions include the niçoise salad with seared tuna and mustard-glazed salmon over mashed potatoes.

Snack Foods
GREAT ATE

THE GREATEST: **Fried Dough**

Big Daddy's $
436 Western Ave., Brighton, MA, (617) 787-1080
www.bdpizza.com
Big Daddy's may be the ultimate cure for the most serious snack attacks. They put a gourmet spin on everything from sandwiches to soups to boneless Buffalo wings. Customers can find fresh baked chocolate chip cookies, toasty pita chips, and pizza slices right out of the oven. Phantom's favorite is the Great White Pie topped with spinach, tomato, mozzarella, and Romano cheese. Big Daddy's specialty is fried dough, puffy bite-sized treats in a basket. Sweet flavors include cinnamon and powdered sugar, while savory versions come coated in butter, garlic, or Parmesan cheese.

THE GREATEST: **Soft Pretzels**

Auntie Anne's $
9 Massachusetts locations
www.auntieannes.com
After a bite-by-bite tour of Auntie Anne's soft pretzel arsenal, Phantom wished he had her as a relative. All of the fresh-baked dough is twisted and tossed with toppings in clear view of the customer. There's a flavor for every craving, whether it's toasted almond, sour cream and onion, jalapeño, or Glazin' Raisin. Cinnamon sugar is the best of the bunch, and it's also available in pretzel sticks by the half dozen. If you're hungry for more, the pretzel dog will do the trick. Throw in some sweet mustard or cheese sauce for dipping, and Phantom is good to go . . . until dinner.

THE GREATEST: **Popcorn**

Dale & Thomas Popcorn $
Faneuil Hall Marketplace, Boston, MA, (617) 725-0090
www.daleandthomas.com
Dale & Thomas is popcorn reinvented. They start with the biggest, fluffiest, tastiest puffed up pieces and then coat them in crazy flavors. Chocolate Chunk N' Caramel comes in clusters bound by dark chocolate. Peanut Butter & White Chocolate DrizzleCorn is salty sweet, and Southwest Cheddar has the heat of smoky chipotle

chiles. Chicken wing fans will love the Buffalo and Blue Popcorn: an indulgent mix of blue cheese and Buffalo wing sauce. But popcorn purists can get their fix, too; the Hall of Fame Kettle Corn is irresistible, sprinkled with sea salt and pure cane sugar.

THE GREATEST: Coffee Cake

Cape Cod Coffee Cakes $$
www.capecodcoffeecakes.com

Cape Cod Coffee Cakes are incredibly rich, with a cinnamon and brown sugar swirl that cuts right through the center. The sour cream cakes are moist and springy, but the best part is the streusel baked on top and bottom. Bass River Blueberry is bursting with fruit, while Martha's Vineyard Marble is perfect for the chocolate addict. For something heartier, there's Woods Hold Walnut Cranberry. The cakes make great gifts, nestled in a beautiful box with a Cape Cod picture on top. Order online or find them at select stores like Pemberton Farms in Cambridge.

THE GREATEST: Homemade Potato Chips

Warren Tavern $
2 Pleasant St., Charlestown, MA, (617) 241-8142
www.warrentavern.com

What do George Washington, Paul Revere, and the Phantom Gourmet have in common? A great love of Warren Tavern, the historic watering hole established in 1780. There's something special about raising a glass in the same place as your forefathers, but most memorable (no disrespect intended) are the tavern's potato chips. These thin, crispy curls are the specialty of the house, fried until they're a deep shade of bronze. The menu is all about bar food, listing half-pound bacon cheeseburgers, grilled kielbasa, and classic BLTs.

THE GREATEST: Breadbasket

Not Your Average Joe's $$
8 Massachusetts locations
www.notyouraveragejoes.com

Not Your Average Joe's locations are in the suburbs, so customers can get city-style food without battling the traffic or shelling out a fortune. Phantom could live on their addictive Tuscan breadbasket alone, which comes with olive oil infused with Parmesan, hot pepper flakes, and garlic. If you can save room, the global menu includes pasta, pizza, salads, and sandwiches. Phantom's favorites are the Voodoo Shrimp and the Black Angus sirloin meatloaf with garlic mashed potatoes. This affordable chain is located in neighborhoods like Arlington, Watertown, Randolph, and Beverly.

THE GREATEST: **Cinnamon Roll**

Cinnabon $

4 Massachusetts Locations

www.cinnabon.com

If you've never had a Cinnabon cinnamon roll, you probably do all of your shopping online. Cinnabon stands are often in malls, where the warm, sugary dough and cream cheese frosting are just the treat you need after a long day of store hopping. The thick regular version is the size of a small child's head, but there are Minibons for smaller appetites and Cinnabon Stix if you prefer to dip in the icing. For a snack that's even nuttier, there's the Caramel Pecanbon.

THE GREATEST: **Chips and Salsa**

On the Border $

19 Commerce Way, Woburn, MA, (781) 938-8990

www.ontheborder.com

On the Border is a fun Tex-Mex chain where the meal kicks off with free chips and salsa. From there, you can keep on snacking with three kinds of queso dip: fajita chicken, chili, or the ultimate loaded with taco meat and refried beans. If guacamole is your weakness, they'll make it at your table with ripe avocados, cilantro, jalapeños, and lime. Phantom always orders a big old margarita and sizzling fajitas made with mesquite-grilled chicken. For dessert, the outrageous Turtle Empanadas explode with hot chocolate from a cinnamon-sugar donut, all topped with caramel and pecans.

Steak
GREAT ATE

THE GREATEST: Cowboy Ribeye

Ruth's Chris Steak House $$$
2513 Berlin Tpk., Newington, Conn., (860) 666-2202
www.ruthschris.com
Ruth's Chris Steak House may have an odd name, but there's nothing confusing about the superior steaks at this Southern-bred chain. Each cut of Prime beef is broiled at 1,800 degrees and finished with a hunk of butter that melts on contact and slides over the edges. The New York strip is well marbled and fiercely flavorful, while the huge Cowboy Ribeye is insanely tender with a deep, meaty taste. New Orleans–style appetizers include the shrimp rémoulade with creamy Creole mustard. Their Boston location is in elegant Old City Hall.

THE GREATEST: Meat Locker

The Capital Grille $$$
359 Newbury St., Boston, MA, (617) 262-8900
www.thecapitalgrille.com
The Capital Grille may be a nationwide chain, but you still get personal attention and all the dry-aged beef you could want. They dry age their beef for two weeks in temperature- and humidity-controlled meat lockers, with incredibly flavorful results. The Kona coffee-crusted Kansas City strip gains complexity from cracked pepper and caramelized onions, and the porcini rubbed Delmonico boasts gorgeous marbling. Everything is over the top, including crème brûlée buried in fresh fruit and a 300-selection wine list. Phantom prefers Chestnut Hill to the Back Bay location for the free valet and VIP treatment. There's a third outpost in Providence.

THE GREATEST: Steak Sauces

Max Stein's American Steakhouse $$$
94 Hartwell Ave., Lexington, MA, (781) 402-0033
www.maxsteins.com
Max Stein's looks like it's straight out of the '40s, but there's nothing old-fashioned about this stylish supper club with a color-changing bar. The menu features an Angus steak slathered in Max's herb butter and a tender bone-in filet finished in Max's signature truffle wine sauce. For an even richer dish, the two-and-a-half pound Lobster

Thermidor is stuffed with scallops and Parmesan cream sauce. Unlike your typical steakhouse, every entrée includes a free twice-baked potato. And the fried banana split is an obscene dessert of homemade ice cream and chocolate sauce plus deep fried bananas rolled in crushed peanuts.

THE GREATEST: New York–Style Steak House

Smith & Wollensky $$$
101 Arlington St., Boston, MA, (617) 423-1112
www.smithandwollensky.com
Smith & Wollensky, a New York–style chain steak house, stands proud in an opulent four-story Armory castle complete with an elevator. Portions (and prices) are obscene, including five-pound lobsters and barbaric cuts of beef like the 28-ounce Colorado rib steak. Also on the picture-framed menu are a mountain of onion rings big enough to feed 10, and 650 selections on the Great American Wine List. They're famous for their split pea soup and a glass-enclosed kitchen table within the main kitchen. Colossal desserts include the smothered ice cream sundae and the ice cream shooters served in a flight of six flavors.

THE GREATEST: Steak and Seafood

Grill 23 & Bar $$$
161 Berkeley St., Boston, MA, (617) 542-2255
www.grill23.com
Grill 23 & Bar perfects the prime steakhouse concept and steps it up with day-boat seafood. The upscale menu includes a fat Kobe beef Delmonico, a massive porterhouse, and wild king salmon with a tamarind BBQ glaze. The only way to start is with the Grill 23 sliders, served on sesame brioche with house-made potato chips. On the side, it's bacon mac and cheese or insanely addictive truffle tater tots. The loud, social lounge buzzes with business mergers and stiff drinks, and the elegant dining room displays massive marble columns and an entourage of chefs' whites in the open kitchen.

THE GREATEST: Modern Steak House

Metropolitan Club $$$
1210 Boylston St., Chestnut Hill, MA, (617) 731-0600
www.metclubandbar.com
The Met Club is so stylish, you might think you've stumbled off the Prime beef path and into a party scene. Actually, it's both. From the blue glass bar to the oversized leather booths, the menu includes modern dishes like duck confit spring rolls with pear sauce. Steaks vary from the juicy skirt steak with sweet-hot pepper jam to

the huge bone-in rib eye for two. Even à la carte sides stray from the steak-house norm with tri-colored Parmesan fries and brown sugar sweet potatoes topped with pecans. Save room for decadent desserts like the Met Cupcake spilling cherries and vanilla pudding from a black forest base.

THE GREATEST: Chateaubriand

Oak Room $$$
Fairmont Copley Plaza, 138 St. James Ave., Boston, MA, (617) 267-5300
www.theoakroom.com

The Oak Room in the Fairmont Copley Plaza is a striking, old-world shrine of refinement with elaborate woodwork, crystal chandeliers, and animal trophies. This luxury steak house spares no expense with butter-rich seafood like crab stuffed mushrooms. For an extra special entrée, get the tuxedo-dressed waiter to roll the Chateaubriand for two right to your table. The thick center-cut tenderloin is sliced right before your eyes and is served with bearnaise and potatoes. Post-meal, it's best to digest in the adjoining martini lounge, where every martini comes with a second pour on ice.

THE GREATEST: Bone-In Filet

Abe & Louie's $$$
793 Boylston St., Boston, MA, (617) 536-6300
www.abeandlouies.com

Abe & Louie's serves the best bone-in filet. It's the specialty of the house, presented in a portobello demi-glace. Phantom recommends topping it off with aged cheddar cheese or Great Hill blue cheese. All of their exquisite Prime steaks come from corn-fed Midwestern beef that's been aged four to five weeks. As for seafood, Phantom likes to start with a luxurious shellfish tower or dig right into a wood-grilled swordfish chop. The open space has all the character of a refined steak house, but it's much louder and livelier than most. In fair weather, the scene spills onto an outdoor patio. The wine list runs deep, and Abe & Louie's shakes a classic martini at the mahogany bar.

Sushi
GREAT ATE

THE GREATEST: Upscale Sushi

Fugakyu $$$
1280 Beacon St., Brookline, MA, (617) 738-1268
www.fugakyu.net

Fugakyu is a beautiful Japanese restaurant staffed by kimono-dressed waitresses. Customers can watch the chefs in action at the conveyer-belt sushi bar, or settle into the maze of the dining room full of private tatami rooms hidden by sliding rice paper doors. Lively fish tanks show off future dinners of mackerel, sea urchin, lobster, and abalone, and the menu lists both traditional fare and modern maki like the sweet potato roll layered with eel and avocado. Customers who aren't into the raw stuff can choose from a long list of sushi with baked and fried ingredients, plus noodles, curry, fried rice, and bento boxes.

THE GREATEST: Rare Sashimi

Uni $$$
370 Commonwealth Ave., Boston, MA, (617) 536-7200
www.cliorestaurant.com

Located down the leopard-print stairs from the celebrated Clio dining room, Uni is a denlike sashimi bar pairing extremely rare ingredients with nearly a dozen fine sakes. Area foodies jockey for a seat at the black marble bar to witness chef Ken Oringer in action. Exotic offerings include sea urchin with quail eggs, kumamoto oysters with Japanese fruit, and lightly battered freshwater eel. Jaw-dropping garnishes like caviar, wasabi foam, or green tea salt make each awesomely expensive bite a delicious indulgence.

THE GREATEST: Toro

Oishii Sushi $$
612 Hammond St., Chestnut Hill, MA, (617) 277-7888
www.oishiisushi.com

Oishii is a snug sushi bar with 10 coveted counter seats where customers can watch the sushi experts slice and roll. It's a bare-basics closet of a room, but there's no better dressed fish in town (or out of town)! Expert sushi chefs craft generous portions of extremely tasty, fresh fish. Phantom goes for the toro, which is the coveted fatty part of the tuna. At Oishii, the salmon shimmers, the red clam comes paper thin, and the spicy scallop hand rolls are sublime. Hot entrées are equally outstanding, with udon noodles and grilled selections that come to the counter sizzling on a hot stone. Additional locations include Sudbury and Boston's South End.

THE GREATEST: Sushi and Scene

Oishii Boston $$$
1166 Washington St., Boston, MA, (617) 482-8868
www.oishiiboston.com

Oishii Sushi (listed above) is arguably the best sushi bar in the area, but it now has some serious competition . . . from itself. Its sister restaurant, Oishii Boston, takes the same fresh approach to maki. The new outpost is way more modern, expansive, and expensive. Past the two-story wall of water, the sleek slate dining room runs along an impossibly long sushi bar lined with seats. Progressive sushi includes tuna cucumber maki spiked with whole-grain mustard instead of wasabi. Seared toro sandwiches melt like butter between crispy rice chips topped with gold leaf, and the "real" California roll features snow crab meat. For an unforgettable appetizer, the Ishiyaki Kobe beef is brought to the table raw, to be cooked by the customer on a stone grill.

THE GREATEST: City-Style Sushi

Douzo $$$
131 Dartmouth St., Boston, MA, (617) 859-8886
www.douzosushi.com

Douzo caught Phantom's eye with its experimental sushi menu and urban décor. The soaring space plays with lines and shapes, and the split-level dining spills from a sleek lounge. Japanese cuisine gets a modern makeover with unusual sushi your chopsticks have never before encountered. The Alligator Roll combines eel, crab, and shrimp tempura, while the pristine yellowtail appetizer teams up with hot jalapeños and yuzu citrus sauce. Some hand rolls skip the rice and wrap with cucumber instead of seaweed. Those who are squeamish about raw fish can order their sushi "torched"—like the toro maki with jalapeño. Or they can skip the fish altogether and order the spareribs.

THE GREATEST: Sushi Buffet

Minado $$
1282 Worcester Rd., Natick, MA, (508) 647-0495
www.minado.com

Phantom was skeptical, too, but the all-you-can-eat sushi buffet at Minado is expansive without compromising quality. The cavernous 360-seat dining room invites seafood lovers to sink their teeth into 100 selections including maki, sashimi, and made-to-order hand rolls. Along with tuna, eel, and yellowtail, there's crab with avocado, fried salmon, and shrimp tempura. During dinner hours, there's also a teppan-yaki grill station where the chef cooks beef, chicken, or vegetables while you wait. Other luxury items include oysters on the half-shell, lobster tails, and giant snow crab legs.

THE GREATEST: Stylish Sushi

Osushi. $$
10 Huntington Ave., Boston, MA, (617) 266-2788
www.osushirestaurant.com
Osushi is Boston's hippest sushi house, flooded by trendy diners sipping flowery sake-tinis infused with Asian pear. The menu is more conservative than the sleek décor, offering traditional Japanese fare and cooked rolls for the squeamish. Miso soup and salad with sesame dressing come with each combination meal, like suzuki (sea bass), chutoro (tuna), and fat Crystal Rainbow Rolls of eel, avocado, and cucumber capped with tuna, whitefish, sake, and tobiko. There's a second Osushi in the Financial District.

THE GREATEST: Spider Maki

Ginza $$$
16 Hudson St., Boston, MA, (617) 338-2261
www.ginzaboston.com
Ginza is *the* Chinatown sushi spot, and it's got great late-night people-watching as the clubbers gather until 4 a.m. With elbow-to-elbow seating, you won't miss any of the action. The house specialty is the Spider Maki—an artfully dramatic roll with amazing crunch and texture. Deep-fried soft-shelled crab, creamy avocado, cucumber, rice, and flying fish roe are wound into giant seaweed slices. Ginza has a second location in Brookline that offers the same perfect sticky rice and tempura green tea ice cream.

Tiny Treasures
GREAT ATE

THE GREATEST: **Affordable Date**

Orinoco $
477 Shawmut Ave., Boston, MA, (617) 369-7075
www.orinocokitchen.com

Orinoco is an affordable tiny treasure that's perfect for a date; the atmosphere is alive with color, and the flavorful Latin food will give you plenty to talk about. Phantom sips a tropical fruit drink while deciding on Venezuelan specialties like empanada pastries stuffed with shredded beef or sandwiches stacked on savory corn bread. The bacon-wrapped dates stuffed with almonds might be the best appetizer in the entire South End, and you can round out the meal with moist adobo chicken and fried sweet plantains.

THE GREATEST: **Artsy Bistro**

café D $$
711 Centre St., Jamaica Plain, MA, (617) 522-9500
www.cafedboston.com

The storefront café D is funky and eclectic, where international newsprint plasters one wall and random artwork draws attention from the mismatched chandeliers. Couples can hide away in the curtained-off bar, feeding each other made-to-order guacamole and chips. The bistro menu swings from Vermont cheddar burgers to the "colossal" turkey leg braised in mole poblano. The specialty of the house is the Moroccan spiced lamb over toasted couscous, but Phantom's favorite is the steak frites drenched in mustard butter. The nightly prix fixe makes three-course dining pretty darn affordable.

THE GREATEST: **Dinner Deal**

Dok Bua Thai Kitchen $
411 Harvard St., Brookline, MA, (617) 277-7087
www.dokbuathai.com

Part grocery store and part restaurant, Dok Bua is 100 percent delicious *and* dirt cheap. The menu reads like a picture book, with photos of all the authentic Thai dishes. The visuals are great for taking the mystery out of ordering som-tom (papaya salad), poo-nim (crispy soft-shell crab), and whole steamed fish. From 5 p.m. to

11 p.m., the unbeatable meal deal includes an entrée like crispy pork, pad-si-ew noodles, or coconut curry, plus sides of jasmine rice, soup, a crispy egg roll, and two-pork dumplings. The even cheaper lunch special (noon to 5 p.m.) includes two sides.

THE GREATEST: Irish Pub

Matt Murphy's Pub $$
14 Harvard St., Brookline Village, MA, (617) 232-0188
www.mattmurphyspub.com

Matt Murphy's is unmistakably Irish, with thick accents, a stand-up bar, and live music most nights. This authentic pub serves superior ales from the brass tap and the best stick-to-your-ribs Irish food in town. The shepherd's pie is especially tasty, with mashed potatoes baked into the top of a chunky lamb stew. Fish and chips is another favorite, served in a newspaper-wrapped bundle with homemade ketchup infused with cinnamon, cumin, and garlic. They also do a pub-style steak cooked in stout sauce and irresistible bread pudding drizzled with caramel.

THE GREATEST: Offbeat Pizzeria

Pizza Oggi $
131 Broad St. Boston, MA, (617) 345-0022

Pizza Oggi starts with light, fluffy dough that's brushed with oil, sesame seeds, and onion flakes. The sauce is homemade, the crust is crispy, and all the toppings receive extra attention from marinating, roasting, or smoking. Even the plain cheese pie goes above and beyond with roasted garlic. If that's too simple, add wild mushrooms, truffle oil, and fresh lobster. Phantom savors the goat cheese pizza with toasted almonds and cherry tomatoes, but the most popular is the Hawaiian pizza with roasted pineapple, smoked ham, and scallions. Peaches and prosciutto? Surprisingly pleasant!

THE GREATEST: Cozy Wine Bar

The Butcher Shop $$$
552 Tremont St., Boston, MA, (617) 423-4800
www.thebutchershopboston.com

The Butcher Shop doubles as a charcuterie store by day and a trendy wine bar by night. The antipasto plate might include homemade sausage, cheese, and marinated olives, and the house hot dog is covered in Gruyère cheese. The lunch menu ventures into pulled pork plates with hot pepper jelly and the best grilled cheese you'll ever eat, upgraded with prosciutto and tomatoes. Past the massive butcher block table in the back, the glass door refrigerator stocks well-marbled beef, farm fresh eggs, and jars of homemade preserves.

THE GREATEST: Spice Pantry

Christina's Spice & Specialty Foods $
1255 Cambridge St., Cambridge, MA, (617) 576-2090
Christina's Spice only occupies a couple of hundred square feet, but every inch is jammed with imported spices. Choose from 40 kinds of chiles, 20 varieties of rice, 15 different dried mushrooms, and a selection of 15 salts that includes Hawaiian pink- and black-smoked Mexican. They even stock 50 botanicals, as well as teas, heirloom beans, avocado leaves, and grains of paradise. The spice store is an off-shoot of Christina's Homemade Ice Cream next door, with inspired flavors like banana cinnamon, fresh mint, carrot cake, and white chocolate lavender.

THE GREATEST: Tiny Trattoria

Daily Catch $$
323 Hanover St., Boston, MA, (617) 523-8567
www.dailycatch.com
Daily Catch is a teeny, tiny trattoria serving sensational seafood. The 20-seat dining room even shares the same space as the kitchen. Nicknamed the "calamari café," Daily Catch offers eight renditions of that Italian delicacy. They're fried, sautéed, steamed, marinated, stuffed, and even rolled into balls. The blackboard menu lists other Sicilian seafood like linguine with clams or monkfish Marsala with mushrooms. Wine and Moretti beer are served in plastic cups. Additional locations include Brookline and Boston's waterfront.

Wings
GREAT ATE

THE GREATEST: **Wing Variety**

The Chicken Bone $
358 Waverly St., Framingham, MA, (508) 879-1138
www.thechickenbone.com
The Chicken Bone is a blues club and a dive bar with the best chicken wing variety
around. Unlike most places, their chicken is always fresh instead of frozen. But the
special treatment doesn't stop there—wings are marinated in buttermilk and secret
spices and dunked in homemade sauces. The two main menu items are boneless
wings and wings with bones, and they both come in flavors like Just Plain Hot, Just
Plain Mild, Honey BBQ, Honey Mustard, and hotter-than-habanero Thermonu-
clear. For a wildly different wing, try the Roman sauce made from Italian dressing,
Parmesan cheese, and garlic.

THE GREATEST: **Caribbean Wings**

Parish Cafe $$
361 Boylston St., Boston, MA, (617) 247-4777
www.parishcafe.com
The Parish Cafe in the Back Bay is known for its signature sandwiches named for and
invented by local celebrity chefs. But Phantom can't get enough of their Roasted Reg-
gae Wings, which might have you blowing off the Buffalo wing forever. These extra
meaty morsels are marinated for 24 hours in soy sauce, citrus, and Jamaican jerk
spices. Then they're baked, not fried, and served with tangy, sweet banana mango
chutney. The Parish also has 11 beers on tap, 50 more by the bottle, 20 magnificent
martinis, and an outdoor patio where Boston's beautiful people love to pass those hot
summer days. If you do stay for a sandwich, the amazing Zuni Roll is a grilled tortilla
stuffed with turkey, bacon, dill Havarti cheese, and cranberry chipotle sauce.

THE GREATEST: **Boneless Buffalo Wings**

Ninety Nine Restaurant & Pub $$
61 Massachusetts locations
www.99restaurants.com
The Ninety Nine Restaurant chain claims to have invented the boneless Buffalo
wing, which is the perfect finger food with a tall, frosty mug of Sam Adams. Juicy

tenders of chicken breast are battered by hand, fried to golden perfection, covered in spicy sauce, and served in traditional fashion with blue cheese dressing and celery sticks. The Ninety Nine also offers Gold Fever Wings dripping in honey-mustard BBQ sauce and honey BBQ wings with a tangy sauce smeared over every boneless inch. The kitchen is truly all-American with entrées like the grilled sirloin, 10-ounce steakburgers, and fish and chips.

THE GREATEST: Wing Delivery

Wing It $
1153 Commonwealth Ave., Allston, MA, (617) 783-BIRD
www.wing-it.com

If you're lazy like Phantom, you don't even have to get off your couch to savor the 21 scrumptious wing flavors from Wing It in Allston. They claim one of the biggest delivery areas around, stretching far into the 'burbs on door-to-door service. The finger-food menu has everything you need for the big game, including burgers, ribs, crinkle-cut fries, and mozzarella sticks. But nothing beats the house specialty wings. Heat seekers love the suicidal Buffalo hots, while the more adventurous opt for addictive Dijon, gooey-sweet honey BBQ, and buttery garlic and Parmesan.

THE GREATEST: Buffalo Wings

Buff's Pub $
317 Washington St., Newton, MA, (617) 332-9134

The large buffalo head mounted on the wall is the first clue that Buff's Pub is serious about wings. Made only from farm fresh chicken that's never frozen, their perfect poultry would probably take flight if not grounded in heavenly sauce. The traditional BBQ wings are extra-thick through the middle and deep-fried to render the joints crunchy. Slightly sweeter versions include honey hot and honey BBQ. Other pub grub includes deep-dish potato skins and beef soft tacos. As an all-American watering hole, Buff's is lined with beer ads and bar stools.

THE GREATEST: Hot Buffalo Wings

Wendell's Pub $
30 West Main St., Norton, MA, (508) 285-5555

Spice addicts flock to the unassuming Wendell's Pub for legendary Buffalo wings offered at varying degrees of heat. Sissy Wings won't even tingle your tongue, but the spice factor builds with Regular, Half & Half, 3.5, Spicy, and crazy hot Suicidal. Double Dare is so darn fiery, it's not even listed on the menu. The kitchen uses a special cooking technique of extended deep-frying for extra crispy results. And they've perfected the "Wendell Flip," ensuring even sauce distribution over every wing.

THE GREATEST: Sweet and Spicy Wings

Audubon Circle $$
838 Beacon St., Boston, MA, (617) 421-1910
Audubon Circle serves its chicken wings in a Chinese take-out box, but this sweet and spicy appetizer won't make it two feet before you're licking the container clean. Sprinkled with sesame seeds and scallions, they're mixed with carrots carved into flowers! The first bite releases sugary ginger notes, but full-on fiery spice quickly kicks in. The menu covers comfort food with originality, like hot pressed sandwiches, pork chops with fried green tomatoes, and juicy burgers with home-made ketchup and golden roasted potatoes. Audubon is practically pitching distance from Fenway Park, so game day brings a slew of Red Sox fans to the slate bar and stylish, urban space.

THE GREATEST: Buffalo Chicken Nachos

The Four's $
166 Canal St., Boston, MA, (617) 720-4455
www.thefours.com
Across from the TD Banknorth Garden, The Four's in Boston and Quincy makes the most delicious Buffalo chicken nachos. Crunchy tortilla chips, mounds of Buffalo chicken, and melted mozzarella combine into a delicious monstrosity that's dotted with hot sauce. True chicken wing fans can dig into traditional Buffalo wings in Louisiana hot sauce or Four's Wings tossed in an Oriental marinade. The Bobby Orr steak and cheese is a house specialty, along with the Carl Yastrzemski pastrami and Swiss sandwich. The Four's is one of the oldest sports bars in the entire nation, and it's packed with authentic jerseys and autographed pictures.

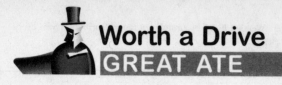

Worth a Drive
GREAT ATE

THE GREATEST: Jewish Deli

Rein's Deli $
345 Hartford Tpk., Vernon, CT, (860) 875-1344
www.reinsdeli.com

Located between Boston and the Big Apple, Rein's makes one delicious road stop. It's as "New York" a deli as you'll find in a suburban strip mall. The half-sour pickles are crisp as can be, and everything, including hot pastrami and classic New York cheesecake, is available from the huge take-out counter. The menu is 100 percent Jewish deli, offering staples like hot brisket, potato pancakes, overstuffed corned beef sandwiches, and bagels with lox and cream cheese. The extensive seating area is decked out with a huge Statue of Liberty and kitschy signs that say things like "sit down and relox."

THE GREATEST: Dinner with a View

Simon Pearce $$$
The Mill, 1760 Main St., Quechee, VT, (802) 295-1470
www.simonpearceglass.com

Simon Pearce is a spectacular setting that overlooks the Ottauquechee River from a restored linen mill. The glass-enclosed terrace is situated right above a waterfall, and the restaurant's dishes and stemware are crafted in the on-site glassblowing shop. Customers can even watch the craftsmen at work. The creative kitchen turns out favorites like crispy duck spring rolls and horseradish-crusted cod stacked between mashed potatoes and fried leeks.

THE GREATEST: Pepperoni Pizza

Pizza Barn $
1860 Rte. 16, Center Ossipee, NH, (603) 539-2234

The Pizza Barn is located in a century-old barn that's two hours from Boston. But Phantom doesn't think twice about the mileage when he's hungry for the best pepperoni pie on the planet. Hand-cut slices of the savory meat are folded into and around the pie until it looks like a mountain of meat. The cheesy disc is then cooked, like all Pizza Barn pizzas, until well done and extra crispy around the edge. They also make a sweet-savory Hawaiian pizza and a towering taco pizza that defies gravity. The biggest of them all is the eight-pound Farmer's Daughter covered in hamburger, pepperoni, mushrooms, onions, and peppers.

THE GREATEST: Specialty Sauces

Stonewall Kitchen Café $
Stonewall Lane, York, ME, (207) 351-2719
www.stonewallkitchen.com/Cafe
Stonewall Kitchen is known for its jam shops and free samples, but Phantom thinks it's worth a drive to their flagship store for a visit to the company's only café. Outdoor seating overlooks the beautiful gardens, and inside the bistro atmosphere is cute and quaint. New England dishes get a flavor boost from Stonewall sauces and dressings. The grilled jumbo shrimp salad comes drizzled with tomato basil vinaigrette, and the Angus beef burger sits on a bulky roll with roasted garlic and onion jam. For an especially hearty entrée, try the crock of lobster pie topped with a cream cheese biscuit.

THE GREATEST: Rustic, Romantic Retreat

The Dunaway Restaurant at Strawberry Banke $$$
66 Marcy St., Portsmouth NH, (603) 373-6112
www.dunawayrestaurant.com
The blazing fireplace and loft seating at the Dunaway Restaurant at Strawberry Banke put Phantom in the mood for New England comfort food. Start with creamy Maine lobster bisque or seared scallops in parsley butter, the biggest Phantom has ever seen. The grilled hanger steak teams up with bacon-infused Brussels sprouts, and the charcuterie plate features the best artisanal cheese in New England. The kitchen takes advantage of an extensive herb garden out back, which is also part of the historic Strawberry Banke Museum.

THE GREATEST: Chocolate Bread

When Pigs Fly $
447 U.S. Rte. 1, Kittery, ME, (207) 439-3114
www.sendbread.com
When Pigs Fly bakes the most extraordinary breads you'll ever eat. Their all-natural, handmade loaves are packed with fresh fruits, nuts, and grains. The one that rises above the others is their chocolate bread. Packed with chocolate chips, it's a rich loaf that's fudgy like a dense dark brownie but light and crusty like any good bread should be. Phantom likes to spread on some peanut butter, fry it up as French toast, or turn it into an ice cream sandwich. Their bread list is 20 flavors deep, including cinnamon raisin, pumpkin date cranberry, sourdough, and multigrain

anadama. It's worth a drive to their retail shop, but you can also get a taste at supermarkets around New England.

THE GREATEST: **High-Stakes Dining**

Paragon $$$
Foxwoods Resort Casino, 39 Norwich-Westerly Rd., Ledyard, CT,
1-800-FOXWOODS
www.foxwoods.com
Located 24 floors above Foxwoods Casino, Paragon hits the fine dining jackpot. It's Phantom's favorite place to blow his bank on lobster and steak, while taking in live piano music and a ceiling set with twinkling "stars." The menu is deluxe continental, offering expensive versions of everything from fried chicken to lamb chops. The Caesar salad is tossed tableside, and the Kobe beef sliders pair with crispy, slender shoestring fries. Every customer wins big with freebies like an *amuse bouche,* an overflowing breadbasket, complimentary cookies, and strawberries that accompany the check.

THE GREATEST: **Cajun and Creole**

Chef Wayne's Big Mamou $$
63 Liberty St., Springfield, MA, (413) 732-1011
One taste of the Cajun and Creole fare at Chef Wayne's Big Mamou, and you'll swear you were in the French Quarter. The specialty of the house is puff pastry baked around crawfish, shrimp, and veggies in lobster cream sauce. Other enormous entrées include shrimp and sausage jambalaya and pork loin stuffed with sausage cornbread filling. Make room for Bourbon Street Cheese Bread and Jerked Thunder Thighs. Surrounded by Louisiana murals and stuffed alligators, Chef Wayne's is all about eating and fun. The menu is BYOB, and some customers bring their own blenders for homemade margaritas!

"GREAT ATES"
by Location

Back Bay
GREAT ATE

THE GREATEST: Prime Steak

Abe & Louie's $$$
793 Boylston St., Boston, MA, (617) 536-6300
www.abeandlouies.com

Abe & Louie's is a fun, animated place for group dining over Prime steaks. Their bone-in filet is the specialty of the house, and it's even better smothered in cheddar cheese. Start with French onion soup or Abe's shellfish tower and then sink into a rich rib eye steak or the most tender filet mignon you'll ever eat. À la carte classics like hashed brown potatoes and creamed spinach get some competition from the jumbo sweet potato baked with brown sugar. Abe & Louie's has a great social scene at the mahogany bar, and their sidewalk patio offers incredible outdoor dining.

THE GREATEST: Celebrity Sandwiches

Parish Cafe $$
361 Boylston St., Boston, MA, (617) 247-4777
www.parishcafe.com

At Parish Cafe, the sandwiches are named after the city's hottest chefs. Local culinary stars submit recipes, so it's possible to eat their top-notch cuisine at a fraction of the price. The most popular is the Cottonwood Café Zuni Roll wrapped around turkey, bacon, and dill Havarti cheese. Chris Schlesinger of East Coast Grill designed a banana nut bread sandwich piled with smoked ham and mango chutney. There's also a BLT with roasted Roma tomatoes on thick buttery Texas Toast and Ming Tsai's "Blue Ginger" with teriyaki tuna and wasabi on scallion focaccia. Parish has sidewalk seating and 60 beers.

THE GREATEST: Mini Burgers

Match $$
94 Massachusetts Ave., Boston, MA, (617) 247-9922
www.matchbackbay.com

Match is Phantom's top pick for cool comfort food. Part restaurant and part lounge, the trendy spot heats up with a 14-foot fireplace in the middle of the wall. Cool martinis like the champagne spiked Bubbletini are served in a mini shaker, and the

Pop Culture cocktail comes in a glass rimmed in candy Pop Rocks. Mini burgers often skip the beef in favor of lobster or sausage, and small plates of chicken satay with peanut sauce and shrimp-chorizo skewers were made for sharing. And since you've been snacking, there's room for lusty desserts like pan-seared cookie dough.

THE GREATEST: Clambake

Jasper White's Summer Shack $$
50 Dalton St., Boston, MA, (617) 867-9955
www.summershackrestaurant.com

Jasper White's Back Bay outpost is a scaled-back version of the Alewife and Mohegan Sun locations. The casual seafood shack offers a packed menu of pan-roasted lobster, smash-your-own Old Bay crabs and several kinds of chowder. Sides like sweet corn fritters with maple syrup are downright delicious, and their corn dog with fries may be the best deal in town. This Summer Shack is also home of the city's largest raw bar, packed with nine kinds of oysters, plus littlenecks, cherrystones, ceviche, and crab claws. Happy hour and late-night menus save Phantom from getting famished between meals.

THE GREATEST: Candy Store

Sugar Heaven $
218 Newbury St., Boston, MA, (617) 266-6969
www.sugarheaven.us

Think you've died and gone to Sugar Heaven? Your sweet dream comes true on Newbury Street, where a wild retro store displays bins of colorful candy crammed between a sky-blue ceiling and a plastic grass floor. Customers shop until midnight for candy novelties like spun-to-order cotton candy and make-your-own Pixie Sticks with flavors including bubble gum, orange cream, and fruit punch. The M&M Colorworks machine dispenses 21 bold shades of milk chocolate at the push of a lever.

THE GREATEST: Lunch Buffet

Kashmir $$
279 Newbury St., Boston, MA, (617) 536-1695
www.kashmirrestaurant.com

Kashmir is an elegant Indian eatery specializing in tandoori dishes baked in a clay oven and curries that range from mild to fiery hot. Minted scallops with saffron are a Phantom favorite, along with crispy samosa pastries stuffed with potato. The expansive lunch buffet is an incredible deal, spread with traditional dishes like chicken tikka masala and coconut tomato soup. There's always fresh baked naan bread and sugary desserts like deep-fried dough balls in syrup. Customers who sit outside below street level can smoke flavored tobacco from a hookah for a reasonable fee.

THE GREATEST: People Watching

Stephanie's On Newbury $$
190 Newbury St., Boston, MA, (617) 236-0990
www.stephaniesonnewbury.com

Stephanie's has the greatest people watching in the entire Back Bay. Their sidewalk seating offers a front row view of Newbury Street's premium shopping. The roaring fireplace draws diners inside to a cozy bistro setting where it's all about stylish comfort food. Think warm goat cheese and roasted garlic on French bread, beer braised short ribs over mashed potatoes, and lobster quesadillas. Stephanie's legendary salads might feature sliced tenderloin or sushi grade tuna, and desserts like the Belgian waffle sundae are exactly the way to splurge.

THE GREATEST: Romantic Restaurant

Casa Romero $$
30 Gloucester St., Boston, MA, (617) 536-4341
www.casaromero.com

Casa Romero is incredibly romantic, complete with a hidden patio that opens on warm summer nights. The authentic Mexican eatery is off the beaten path with its alley entrance. Tucking into the colorful tiled space with tin lamps, it's only natural to crave fruity sangria or an authentic margarita. Traditional cooking includes Baja-style fish tacos and chicken flautas with homemade guacamole and sour cream. Chef's specialties include pulled chicken enchiladas smothered in mole poblano and a sweet-smoky dish of pork tenderloin in orange chipotle pepper sauce.

Beacon Hill
GREAT ATE

THE GREATEST: Italian

Grotto $$
37 Bowdoin St., Boston, MA, (617) 227-3434
www.grottorestaurant.com

This tiny eatery may be tucked away at basement level, but it's the best Italian cuisine on the block. The "nightly fixe" is a great three-course deal with tempting options like sweet potato ravioli in sage brown butter or potato gnocchi with braised short ribs and Gorgonzola. The Caped Critic loves their balsamic dipped Kobe steak served with crispy Parmesan fries, and the melting chocolate cake is one decadent dessert topped with vanilla ice cream. Grotto gets artsy with brick walls, velvet draperies, and exposed pipes, so it's perfect for a romantic meal or a fashionable lunch with your favorite politician.

THE GREATEST: Persian Cuisine

Lala Rokh $$
97 Mt. Vernon St., Boston, MA, (617) 720-5511
www.lalarokh.com

The romantic Lala Rokh seduces its diners with cozy rooms and aromatic Persian cuisine. Dishes are woven together with Mediterranean specialties like fenugreek, saffron, and pomegranate, plus exotic herbs, fruits, and nuts. Phantom loves the roasted eggplant and lentil appetizer finished with yogurt and mint. Chutneys like the mango-tamarind spread give the grilled kebobs of veal, lamb, and beef a flavorful counterpart, and authentic desserts like lime-rosewater sorbet topped with crispy noodles round out the exotic meal.

THE GREATEST: Fine Dining

No. 9 Park $$$
9 Park St., Boston, MA, (617) 742-9991
www.no9park.com

No. 9 Park overlooks the Boston Common from a nineteenth-century mansion. The dining area is high-end elegant, with a powerful clientele sinking into marble-topped tables. The best way to experience the first-class European cuisine is with a tasting menu of up to nine courses. Their homemade pastas include the most tender gnocchi you'll ever eat, and the kitchen experiments with successes like the Maine crab salad with squash sorbet. No. 9 boasts one of the best cheese trays in the city. Their hot-spot sister restaurants include B&G Oysters Ltd. and The Butcher Shop, both in the South End.

THE GREATEST: Wine Bar

Bin 26 Enoteca $$
26 Charles St., Boston, MA, (617) 723-5939
www.bin26.com

Bin 26 Enoteca is all about wine. The 20-page vintage list includes a glossary of terms and in-depth descriptions of the grapes. Still, you won't find uptight atmosphere; it's fun and fit for a trendy crowd, with decorations that include a cork collection, a wall of wine labels, and a ceiling of suspended bottles in the bathroom. All that sipping calls for snacks, and the Mediterranean menu delivers with antipasti spreads of Italian cheese and cured meats. Bigger plates include crispy prosciutto baked around fresh mozzarella and scallop-stuffed ravioli.

THE GREATEST: Beacon Hill Breakfast

Panificio $
144 Charles St., Boston, MA, (617) 227-4340
www.panificioboston.com

With the Beatles and the Beach Boys setting the mood and picture windows facing Charles Street, Panificio is the kind of place that will make you late for work. Customers order at the counter, but servers bring the food to your table, guided by portable numbers assigned to each guest. A small but solid breakfast menu focuses on eggs and omelets, and the counter displays a tempting selection of baked breads and pastries. The lunch menu turns to salads and sandwiches, and the dinner crowd is treated to candlelight and more serious fare like steak au poivre with potatoes.

THE GREATEST: Coffee Shop

The Paramount $$
44 Charles St., Boston, MA, (617) 720-1152
www.paramountboston.com

Representing as the neighborhood coffee shop, the Paramount keeps it casual with cafeteria-style service and griddle cuisine that everyone loves. Their golden grilled "3" cheese is Phantom's favorite, stuffed with ham or tomato. Along with breakfasts like malted waffles and blue cheese-bacon omelets, the Paramount does burgers, buttermilk fried chicken, and a mean tuna melt. It's stylish and modern with patches of brick, gallery art, and polished silver seats. The mood turns upscale at night with linen-dressed tables and full service.

THE GREATEST: Bar Scene

Harvard Gardens $$$
316 Cambridge St., Boston, MA, (617) 523-2727
www.harvardgardens.com
The singles scene in Beacon Hill is alive, well, and well fed at the Gardens. The space oozes class, from the hardwood floors to the candlelit banquettes. And a sleek bar stretches the dining room, serving inventive cocktails until 2 a.m. Specializing in modern comfort food, the kitchen caters to a yuppie crowd with steak and cheese "spring rolls," salted edamame and truffle Parmesan fries. Dinner options span from prosciutto pizza to pan-seared sirloin with horseradish mashed potatoes. Even the burger goes cutting edge with spicy "frizzled" onions.

THE GREATEST: Thin-Crust Pizza

Upper Crust $
20 Charles St., Boston, MA, (617) 723-9600
www.theuppercrustpizzeria.com
The Upper Crust turns out Phantastic thin-crust pizza using fresh toppings. Communal dining and counter service make this pizzeria the perfect place to grab a slice as you stroll the boutiques of Charles Street. Neapolitan-style pies have 30 toppings. The crispy MGH Pizza combines spinach and chopped broccoli with feta and tomatoes. Also outstanding, the sesame crusted calzone is impossibly cheesy, loaded with mozzarella, ricotta, and Asiago cheeses; Phantom's go-to add-ons are Canadian bacon and pineapple. The Upper Crust is also in Coolidge Corner, Newbury Street, Lexington, and Hingham.

Cambridge
GREAT ATE

THE GREATEST: **Smart Food**

Miracle of Science Bar + Grill $
321 Mass. Ave., Cambridge, MA, (617) 868-2866

Miracle of Science attracts MIT brainiacs for burgers and brews, but you don't need a PhD to order the pub grub "elements" listed like a Periodic Table. The turkey chipotle chili and steak skewers with apricot chutney are delicious experiments, and the plump jalapeño burger is smothered in pepper jack cheese and tomato-onion ketchup. Instead of fries, try the "potato side" of spicy red bliss wedges pan fried until crispy and hot. Phantom isn't sure what's smarter: the clientele or the space. Lab tabletops and geometric sound pads are cooler than liquid nitrogen.

THE GREATEST: **Exotic Appetizers**

Oleana $$$
134 Hampshire St., Cambridge, MA, (617) 661-0505
www.oleanarestaurant.com

Oleana's Arabic menu is bursting with aromatic spices. Entrées like sea scallops with tangerine butter are outstanding. But Phantom plays to the kitchen's strength and makes a meal out of appetizers. Start with deviled eggs or a chopped salad mixed with walnuts and yogurt dressing. Bread spreads like warm buttered hummus are so good, you'll devour an entire loaf. On the hot side, fried mussels are fired up with hot peppers, and nutty sesame seeds dot the herb-infused olives. Phantom's absolute favorite is the fork-tender Sultan's Delight of tamarind glazed beef and smoky eggplant puree.

THE GREATEST: **Bar Food**

Garden at the Cellar $$
991 Massachusetts Ave., Cambridge, MA, (617) 230-5880
www.gardenatthecellar.com

Described as a "gastropub," the basement-level Garden is top shelf compared to your basic bar. Potted plants and herbs alert the senses that the food is fresh off the local farm. Still, these grown-up guilty pleasures are far from pretentious; the chef is a master at morphing them out of childhood favorites, and at fair prices. Mini burgers sink into brioche buns, nostalgic tater tots are homemade, and the steak frites upgrades with rosemary-truffle fries and parsnip puree. The grilled cheese is properly plated with tomato soup for dipping, but it's herb infused and pampered with sharp cheddar.

THE GREATEST: Cheese

Formaggio Kitchen $$
244 Huron Ave., Cambridge, MA, (617) 354-4750
www.formaggiokitchen.com
Formaggio Kitchen is a gourmet grocery with the best cheese counter in the entire country. Their 400 varieties of funky fromage include 20 kinds of goat cheese, creamy Brie, and more blues than a jazz club. The educated staff will give any customer a tour of the cheese cave, and samples are always spread around the store. Moving toward the bins of rare fruits and vegetables, the tight space is packed to the picture windows with imported jams, oils, wine, and olives. Just don't skip over Boston's best chocolate section, where housemade truffles sit beside the bakery's own granola.

THE GREATEST: Dive

Charlie's Kitchen $
10 Eliot St., Cambridge, MA, (617) 492-9646
Charlie's Kitchen is just what the hangover doctor ordered. Smack in the middle of Harvard Square, this dinerlike dive bar serves up greasy eats like their famous "double cheeseburger." Served open-faced with not one but two patties on a bulky roll, options include spicy chili and pineapple Hawaiian. Jalapeño poppers and beer-battered steak fries round out the offerings, along with Buffalo wings and 48 beers. Charlie's isn't the cleanest place in Cambridge, but it may be the cheapest. The eclectic "people energy" is just as interesting upstairs.

THE GREATEST: Thai

Sugar & Spice $$
1933 Massachusetts Ave., Cambridge, MA, (617) 868-4200
www.sugarspices.com
Sugar & Spice bolsters the Porter Square dining scene with bright, cheery digs and an expert Thai kitchen. The blue tiled walls and colorful lighting give the atmosphere a retro look that's fun and playful. The meals are inexpensive and come to the table fast thanks to the eager-to-please staff. Start with crunchy chicken Thai rolls or pan-fried dumplings before diving into spicy Drunken Noodles in hot basil sauce. The range of coconut curries includes mango and avocado versions, and Crying Tiger is for beef lovers, pairing grilled steak and sticky rice.

THE GREATEST: Bistro

The Rendezvous $$
502 Massachusetts Ave., Cambridge, MA, (617) 576-1900
www.rendezvouscentralsquare.com
You might recognize the skylights in this former Burger King site, but the Rendezvous has transformed the space into a lovely everyday bistro. Feel pampered and well fed from a kitchen that takes a market approach. Fresh results include chilled lobster in an avocado-citrus salad. Skillet-roasted skate in sage brown butter is the house specialty, but Phantom can't resist the honey-almond roast chicken with couscous. The comfortable, low bar is extra deep so there's plenty of room for dining on desserts like warm chocolate cake with hazelnut pralines and cinnamon cream.

THE GREATEST: Zen Dining

OM Restaurant & Lounge $$$
92 Winthrop St., Cambridge, MA, (617) 576-2800
www.omrestaurant.com
OM is a palace of Eastern energy where guests are greeted by a waterfall wall that leads to a stylish lounge. Instead of a boring breadbasket, diners start with Parmesan popcorn. For entrées, try the surf 'n turf, pairing grilled yellowfin tuna with short rib dumplings. Wash it all down with an aromatherapy martini, which infuses essential oils to arouse the senses. Desserts include the flourless chocolate "pâté" and an unusually delicious ice cream sandwich constructed from carrot cake, parsnip ice cream, and habanero caramel.

Chinatown
GREAT ATE

THE GREATEST: Regional Chinese

Jumbo Seafood $$
7 Hudson St., Boston, MA, (617) 542-2823

Jumbo Seafood is Phantom's favorite place for regional Chinese cuisine. Customers choose their own dinner by pointing at a huge fish tank where lobsters, crabs, eel, conch, jellyfish, and giant clams are waiting to be sent to the wok. Most dishes are breaded and fried Hunan-style, served with light sauces like black bean or soy ginger scallion. Jumbo has spicy Szechuan dishes, sweet and sour specialties, and Cantonese delicacies like shark's fin soup. It's inexpensive and open until 2 a.m.

THE GREATEST: Shabu Shabu

Shabu-Zen $$
16 Tyler St., Boston, MA, (617) 292-8828
www.shabuzen.com

Shabu-Zen specializes in Japanese cooking called shabu shabu, in which customers cook their meat, seafood, and veggies in a personal hot pot built right into the table. The spicy kimchi broth is best for lamb or Prime rib eye, while the lemongrass broth is suited to scallops, shrimp, and salmon. Mix your own dipping sauce with soy, garlic, scallions, and red chilies. All orders include noodles or jasmine rice, plus chilled red bean soup for dessert.

THE GREATEST: Dumplings

King Fung Garden $
74 Kneeland St., Boston, MA, (617) 357-5262

King Fung Garden may be a closet-sized hole-in-the-wall, but their cheap Chinese dishes include legendary Peking ravioli. The perfect little dumplings are pan-fried and steamed, served with fiery chili soy sauce. The crispy wontons are just as delicious, with doughy goodness around a pork nugget. Mongolian fire pots are a house specialty, along with rice cakes, pea-pod stems, and the three-course Peking duck that requires 24-hours notice to prepare.

Ginza $$$
16 Hudson St., Boston, MA, (617) 338-2261
www.ginzaboston.com
Ginza is a stark setting of blond wood latticework, with elbow-to-elbow seating
and a sushi bar toward the back. On Fridays and Saturdays, enjoy late-night people
watching as the clubbers converge until the 3:30 a.m. closing. Of their 50 sushi se-
lections, the house specialty is the dramatic Spider Maki with fried soft-shell crab
spiking out of a tight avocado-rice roll. Also a hit, the sizzling beef teriyaki comes
to the table on a stone grill. Ginza's second location in Brookline serves the same
menu, including tempura green tea ice cream.

THE GREATEST: **Chinese Bakery**

Eldo Cake House $
36 Harrison Ave., Boston, MA, (617) 350-7977
Eldo Cake House is Phantom's favorite stop for Chinese baked goods. The light,
tasty sponge cakes are not as sweet as the typical American version, and they're
stuffed with fresh fruit like peach, strawberry, or mango. Coconut buns, iced wal-
nut rolls, and chestnut cakes round out the pastry roll call, and Eldo's custard tarts
have an incredibly flaky crust. Savory cravings can be satisfied with a BBQ pork
bun or a thick rice congee breakfast that could fuel an entire day hiking the Free-
dom Trail. Hard-to-find Asian candies fill countless bins in the adjoining shop, with
samples so you can taste before you buy.

THE GREATEST: **Exotic Atmosphere**

Penang $$
685 Washington St., Boston, MA, (617) 451-6373
www.2nite.com/penang
Not all Asian places in Chinatown are Chinese. Penang is one of the most attractive
eateries, with a rustic hut motif of bamboo canopies and rope walls. The rich décor
is matched by an exotic menu of Malaysian cuisine that works ginger, garlic, and
chili peppers into sometimes-spicy dishes. Phantom starts with a watermelon drink
and some crispy egg-onion pancakes served with curry chicken dipping sauce.
Skewers of beef satay come with sweet-salty peanut sauce, and Tom Yam rice noodles swim with fresh seafood in a delightful lemongrass broth.

THE GREATEST: Hong Kong–Style Seafood

Peach Farm $$
4 Tyler St., Boston, MA, (617) 482-1116

Peach Farm gets packed with non-English-speaking aficionados who know their noodles. Dishes include perfect egg rolls and sumptuous hot and sour soup, but the kitchen's specialty is Hong Kong–style seafood. Choose from walnut shrimp, salted squid, and rarities like sesame jellyfish. Twin lobsters wok-fried in ginger and scallions are a real crowd pleaser, and if you order the pan-seared flounder, the cook will emerge from the kitchen to get your approval on the fish before it's cooked.

THE GREATEST: Vegetarian

Buddha's Delight $
3 Beach St., Boston, MA, (617) 451-2395

Buddha's Delight offers a unique cuisine that contains no animal products. Still, meatfree items like "duck" stir-fry, vermicelli with BBQ "pork," and "beef" chow foon are made with wheat and tofu that imitate the texture and taste of the real deal. Vegetarians experience the rare menu freedom to order from 100 selections, which includes lots of Chinese and Vietnamese options, fruit shakes, noodles, and hot pots. There's a second meatfree location in Brookline.

North End Restaurants

THE GREATEST: Mix-and-Match Pasta

Giacomo's $$
355 Hanover St., Boston, MA, (617) 523-9026

Giacomo's is a tiny trattoria where any combo of mussels, calamari, scallops, and shrimp can be worked into a heap of linguini. Sauces include pesto, marinara, fra diavolo, and lobster pink sauce. House specialties include lobster ravioli and the addictive fried calamarí served with fried hot pepper chips. Lines form early, and the small space gets crowded, but diners who stay the course are rewarded with one of the best values in the North End. Their second location in the South End adds valet parking and desserts like the chocolate tartufo ice cream ball.

THE GREATEST: Mob Scene

Strega $$$
379 Hanover St., Boston, MA, (617) 523-8481
www.stregaristorante.com

Strega gives the North End creative Italian cooking and glittery décor. It's so flashy, it draws celebrities like John Travolta, Vincent "Big Pussy" Pastore from *The Sopranos,* and David Ortiz. The look is trendy and fun, with bold yellow backlighting and flat-screen TVs playing mob movies like *The Godfather*. Still, the main attraction is modern Italian food like several kinds of risotto and pennette pasta tubes with salmon and vodka sauce. Phantom loves their homemade mozzarella and their calamari, which comes marinated and grilled or deep-fried.

THE GREATEST: Peruvian-Italian Fusion

Taranta $$$
210 Hanover St., Boston, MA, (617) 720-0052
www.tarantarist.com

The neighborhood is known for pasta and pizza, but Taranta takes a delicious detour by fusing Peruvian and Italian flavors into one exquisite cuisine. It's a fascinating marriage of hot-sweet chili infusions and Mediterranean fare that's full of seafood, spice, pasta, and root vegetables. Phantom's favorite is the brined pork chop with a sugarcane-rocoto red pepper glaze, caramelized onions, and a yucca cake. The saffron-butter-basted trout is just as exotic, served with giant Peruvian corn. The inviting atmosphere is rustic and charming with exposed brick walls and clay dishes delivered straight out of the oven to the table.

THE GREATEST: Tailor-Made Meals

Dom's $
10 Bartlett Place, Boston, MA, (617) 367-8979
Hidden down a sidestreet, Dom's is perfectly positioned for family dining. The dizzying Italian menu is a whopping 18 pages long, but most customers defer to Dom, who likes to invite himself to the table and ask what you're in the mood to eat. The owner's amazing service doesn't stop there: Dom waits tables, hustles in the kitchen, and sees to it that everyone in the house is happy. The restaurant caters to the kiddies, too, offering complimentary spaghetti and meatballs to anyone under 12.

THE GREATEST: Wine Bar

Enoteca Bricco $$$
241 Hanover St., Boston, MA, (617) 248-6800
www.bricco.com
Enoteca Bricco is a low-key wine bar with candlelit dining and windows that open onto Hanover Street in the summer. The wood-burning oven fires away in the exhibition kitchen, and the granite bar is backed by a wall of Italian wine. Bricco is exorbitantly expensive, but dishes like sausage-and-roast-chicken-stuffed ravioli are an incredibly tasty way to blow your bank. The Prime beef tenderloin is grilled to perfection and served with butternut squash, and the Kobe beef risotto with basil ragu enters flavorful territory that no taste buds have ever explored before.

THE GREATEST: Undiscovered Restaurant

Prezza $$$
24 Fleet St., Boston, MA, (617) 227-1577
www.prezza.com
Prezza draws a word-of-mouth crowd for rustic Italian cuisine that's fit for Phantom. You'll forget the touristy throngs just a couple blocks away when you relax into Prezza's discreet setting. Regulars check in at the friendly, buzzing bar before sitting down to Mediterranean dishes like balsamic figs bundled with Gorgonzola and prosciutto. The unforgettable steak and eggs appetizer pairs a pan-seared tenderloin with a fried egg under porcini cream, and wood-grilled specialties include the cider-glazed double-thick pork loin with chestnut polenta.

THE GREATEST: Pizza and Wine Bar

Nebo $$
90 North Washington St., Boston, MA, (617) 723-6326
www.nebopizzeria.com

Nebo is a classy pizzeria with a commendable wine list, too. This deliciously styl-
ish addition to the North End is the only restaurant in the neighborhood with a Hip
Hop and dance soundtrack. Celebrity chefs and rockers like Peter Wolf and Steven
Tyler are regulars, so there's the added possibility of superstar sightings while
you're unwinding with a nice Chianti. Celebrities aside, the upscale slices are rea-
son enough to pop in. Phantom's favorite pie is the Christina with sausage and
corn, but he's also in love with the arancini rice balls stuffed with mushrooms,
cheese, and honey.

THE GREATEST: Sicilian Steal

Galleria Umberto $
289 Hanover St., Boston, MA, (617) 227-5709

Galleria Umberto is an incredible find that's hit hard during their lunch-only hours.
The cafeteria-style eatery stays open until the Sicilian food runs out, so go early for
the best selection of golden calzones. Rectangular slices of plain cheese pizza
come on a thick, chewy crust, and deep-fried rice balls hide a delicious jackpot of
peas and gravy. The price is right with every item costing less than a five spot, and
tiny Dixie cups of table wine are perfect for the honest, authentic Italian fare.

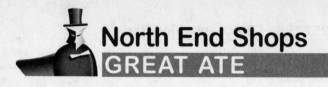

North End Shops
GREAT ATE

THE GREATEST: Gelato

Gelateria $
272 Hanover St., Boston, MA, (617) 720-4243
www.gelateriacorp.com
Gelateria offers a mind-boggling menu of authentic Italian gelato. This creamy treat is denser and more custardlike than ice cream. The psychedelic atmosphere stands out from the rest of Hanover Street, with a flat-screen TV and color-changing LED walls. All-natural ingredients are flown in from Italy and worked into 50 flavors. Phantom's favorites are chocolate, pistachio, and sweet tiramisu. Tart grapefruit, wild cherry, and cantaloupe are unusually delicious, and for two desserts in one, try the gelato-stuffed cannoli. Gelateria is open until midnight every day.

THE GREATEST: Coffee Selection

Polcari's Coffee Shop $
105 Salem St., Boston, MA, (617) 227-0786
www.northendboston.com/polcaricoffee
Polcari's is the best place to buy roasted coffee beans. This old-world shop is lined with creaky wooden floors and offers 30 coffee options that they'll grind on the spot or bag as whole beans. They sell an impressive range of rice, grains, tea, and dried beans. Polcari's is also a dried herb and spice emporium, stocking 100 different varieties like Greek oregano and licorice root. During summer there's lemon slush offered outside the door, where you scoop it yourself and pay by the honor system.

THE GREATEST: Candy Shop

Dairy Fresh Candies $
57 Salem St., Boston, MA, (617) 742-2639
www.dairyfreshcandies.com
This marvelous store carries an incredible selection of candies, including rare Italian varieties. The first room is one crowded aisle of bagged Root Beer Barrels, lemon drops, toffee, caramels, and Mary Janes. The adjoining room features a candy counter stocked with fudge, nuts, and chocolate-dipped pretzels. Hard candy

Perugina flavors include mint, coffee, eggnog, and tangerine. Dairy Fresh also sells licorice chips, gummy candy, Baci chocolates, and candy-coated cinnamon sticks. While combating your sugar craving, stock your kitchen pantry with baking supplies, flavored oils, and exotic dried fruits like papaya.

THE GREATEST: Italian Grocery Store

Salumeria Italiana $$
151 Richmond St., Boston, MA, (617) 523-8743
www.salumeriaitaliana.com

By far the best Italian grocery store, Salumeria Italiana sells imported salami, Prosciutto di Parma, and every cut of pasta imaginable. The flavor-packed olives are cured in brine for months, and the best selection of cheese is available every Friday, when the shipment arrives from Italy. There's also Sicilian sea salt, basil and sun-dried tomato pesto, and red sauce made with capers and chili peppers. The olive oils range from light yellow to dark green, and special slipper-shaped ciabatta bread is available on Saturday. Counter clerks encourage tasting before buying, so you're sure to be pleased with your purchase.

THE GREATEST: Pastry Selection

Mike's Pastry $
300 Hanover St., Boston, MA, (617) 742-3050
www.mikespastry.com

Mike's Pastry has a legendary following, and for good reason: their awe-inspiring Italian pastry selection. The spacious shop has enough room for café seating—a rarity in the North End. Top sellers include the Munchkin-sized boconnotto cream puff, soft baba rum cakes, and the ring-shaped taralli cookies, which come plain or sugar-coated. Also available in massive quantities are cookies, cakes, and marzipan modeled into mini bananas and watermelons. Mike's sells a couple thousand cannoli every day in flavors like ricotta, yellow cream, chocolate cream, chocolate-dipped, and chocolate chip.

THE GREATEST: Traditional Italian Pastry

Maria's Pastry Shop $
46 Cross St., Boston, MA, (617) 523-1196
www.northendboston.com/marias

Maria's Pastry Shop keeps old-world tradition alive by making traditional treats like sfogliatelle. The flaky, layered pastry is shaped like a clam shell, and is filled with creamy cheese and citron fruit. This sugary sweet and rich staple is standard breakfast fare in Naples. The menu expands with cannoli, nougat called torrone and crispelli, and the Italian version of crepes. They stay true to seasonal Italian specialties like ricotta wheat pie at Christmas, Easter egg bread with hard-boiled eggs baked right into the dough, and marzipan lambs and zeppolo donuts on March 19 for St. Joseph's Day.

THE GREATEST: Fresh Mozzarella

Fresh Cheese Shop $
81 Endicott St., Boston, MA, (617) 570-0007
www.northendboston.com/freshcheese

Making homemade ricotta and mozzarella daily, the Fresh Cheese Shop also sells 15 kinds of imported provolone and eight special grated cheeses. There's everything from the popular Parmigiano-Reggiano to Double Gloucester with chives and onions. The staff is happy to assemble an antipasto platter of Italian cold cuts, including any of the sausages dangling above the counter. Every inch of the tiny storefront is in use, including the shelf-lined walls packed with Italian pantry items, 15 kinds of olive oil, and fine balsamic vinegars.

THE GREATEST: Prepared Foods

Monica's Mercato $
130 Salem St., Boston, MA, (617) 742-4101
www.monicasfoods.com

Monica's is the family business running Monica's Restaurant on Richmond Street and Monica's Trattoria on Prince Street. Their homemade pastas and crusty pizzas are awesome, but you can buy these exact items for home cooking at Monica's Mercato, their tiny, charming grocery across the North End. Stop in for homemade sausage, mini calzones, crusty loaves of bread, and fresh ravioli with the house sauce. Prepared foods like lasagna, eggplant Parm, and meatballs make home entertaining easy, and panini sandwiches feature imported cold cuts and cheeses.

South End

THE GREATEST: Roasted Chicken

Hamersley's Bistro $$$
553 Tremont St., Boston, MA, (617) 423-2700
www.hamersleysbistro.com

Hamersley's Bistro is fine dining, but you don't have to dress up to enjoy it. The country French setting is perfectly comfortable for tucking into New England seafood stews, pumpkin risotto, and peppered tuna with almonds and mint. Succulent roasted chicken reigns as the house specialty, surrendering garlic, lemon, and parsley in every moist, delicious bite. Desserts are just as exquisite, like the apple cinnamon croustade spiked with fresh thyme. The open kitchen provides a clear shot of chef Gordon Hamersley sporting his signature Red Sox cap.

THE GREATEST: Blueberry Pancakes

Mike's City Diner $
1714 Washington St., Boston, MA, (617) 267-9393

Mike's City Diner ladles out the city's best pancakes, embedded with blueberries, bananas, and raspberries. These gooey, plate-wide discs are layered in fat, fluffy short stacks with sweet-tart patches of fruit. The rest of the American breakfast menu sizzles with eggs, waffles, and smokin' pork sausage. Phantom loves the homemade hash made from hearty potato cubes and succulent corned beef, finished with two fried eggs. For lunch, the turkey sandwich with french fries is a toasted, meaty classic. As customers enter the luncheonette, they make their way past counter stools alongside the griddle kitchen to the black-and-white checked tabletops.

THE GREATEST: Sleek Scene

Mistral $$$
223 Columbus Ave., Boston, MA, (617) 867-9300
www.mistralbistro.com

Mistral sweeps diners off their feet with unbelievable Mediterranean fare that's still down to earth. Their thin-crust pizza appetizer served with smoky chili oil is grilled-to-order with luxury toppings like tomato, mozzarella, and oregano. The incredibly tender braised beef short ribs comes with roasted garlic mash, and the delicate tuna tartare comes with crispy wontons. For dessert, their cream puff prof-iteroles are out of this world, stuffed full of vanilla ice cream. Every bite goes down in a soaring space that's reminiscent of a farmhouse, but made over with city style. Terra-cotta floors and mini cypress trees add a dramatic edge, while Boston's hottest beefcakes and cupcakes meet and mingle at the bar.

THE GREATEST: Hash

Charlie's Sandwich Shoppe $

429 Columbus Ave., Boston, MA, (617) 536-7669

No one feeds a hash fix like Charlie's Sandwich Shoppe. Forget the beef; this jumbo cake of ground turkey and potatoes is ribboned with onions and carrots and buried beneath two fried eggs. Charlie's serves up breakfast all day from behind a long, swivel stool counter. The greasy spoon décor includes historic Boston photos, glass domes hovering over apple pies or tall Boston cream pies, and communal ta-bles. Other Phantom favorites are the French toast with cranberry syrup and the fluffy blueberry pancakes.

THE GREATEST: $1 Tapas

Masa $$

439 Tremont St., Boston, MA, (617) 338-8884

www.masarestaurant.com

Masa is the exception to the rule in the swank South End, offering bargain food and a hot and spicy scene. The copper bar is inviting for cocktails, and you can also score $1 Southwest tapas after 5 p.m. Of the 10 options on the tapas menu, Phantom fa-vors the steak and guacamole, the chorizo with cranberry chutney, chicken taquitos, shrimp ceviche, and empanadas. For extra savings and an all-around sampling, order the $15 combo platter, which includes a pitcher of sangria. Masa has a selection of over 60 tequilas, which pair well with the strong Latin flavors in the food.

THE GREATEST: Itty-Bitty Brunch Spot

Metropolis Café $

584 Tremont St., Boston, MA, (617) 247-2931

Metropolis Café is a tiny tin of a neighborhood restaurant with one of the city's best brunches. Served on Saturday and Sunday, this memorable meal includes grilled blueberry pancakes and apple chicken sausage. The cranberry pancakes are spectacular, the creamy grits come with fried eggs, and the huevos rancheros are especially delicious, balanced over cumin-spiced black bean hash. Customers squeeze into the tightly spaced tables and wrap around the stool-lined bar, while jazz and star lamps float overhead.

THE GREATEST: Pizza and Ice Cream

PICCO $$
513 Tremont St., Boston, MA, (617) 927-0066

Short for "pizza and ice cream company," PICCO serves the two childhood favorites in a way any adult can appreciate. On the ice cream side, expect small batches made from ingredients like Scharffen Berger chocolate, Kona coffee, and Madagascar vanilla bean. Pizzas are just as premium, topped with housemade sausage or combos like spinach and goat cheese. There's also the Alsatian Variation finessed with bacon, onion, sour cream, and Gruyère cheese. The trendy décor puts an updated spin on the ice cream parlor with cherry-colored chairs and trailing votives.

THE GREATEST: Classy Comfort Food

Union Bar and Grille $$$
1357 Washington St., Boston, MA, (617) 423-0555
www.unionrestaurant.com

Union Bar and Grille turns out urban comfort food for the stylish soul. The menu gets creative with dishes like sweet corn risotto with chorizo sausage and fire roasted peppers. The potato gnocchi are smothered in cream and smoked bacon, and the meal kicks off with skillet cornbread. Almost every one of their delicious desserts is capped with homemade ice cream in wild flavors like Marcona almond, ginger, or blood orange. The renovated warehouse has an urban atmosphere combining massive wrought-iron chandeliers and black leather banquettes, and the dark lounge is framed in floor-to-ceiling glass and slanted mirrors.

Theater District
GREAT ATE

THE GREATEST: **Bar Food**

Avila $$$
1 Charles St. South, Boston, MA, (617) 267-4810
www.avilarestaurant.com

Avila is a hot spot for Mediterranean-style fine dining, but their best feature may be the huge boat-shaped bar. This more casual menu is meant for sharing. Fancy finger foods include Kobe beef pizza and cheesesteak spring rolls with spicy homemade ketchup. Truffle fries upgrade the River Rock beef burger, and the lamb tenderloin pita pocket is rich and satisfying, topped with feta cheese and Greek yogurt. When Phantom wants comfort food, it's the fettuccine carbonara in bacon cream sauce that catches his eye. Avila also puts on a great Sunday brunch with dishes like caramel almond pancakes.

THE GREATEST: **Steak**

Smith & Wollensky $$$
101 Arlington St., Boston, MA, (617) 423-1112
www.smithandwollensky.com

Smith & Wollensky, a New York–style chain steak house has so many floors, you have to take an elevator to each opulent dining room. Portions (and prices) are obscene, including five-pound lobsters and barbaric cuts of beef like the 28-ounce Colorado rib steak. The mountain of onion rings is big enough to feed 10 people, and the Great American Wine List goes 650 selections deep. They're famous for split pea soup and colossal desserts like the ice cream sundae with candy toppings and frozen bananas dipped in chocolate, caramel, butterscotch, or raspberry coulis. For a special treat, request a table in the chef's room where diners get a great view of the kitchen in action.

THE GREATEST: **Group Dining**

P. F. Chang's $$
8 Park Plaza, Boston, MA, (617) 573-0821
www.pfchangs.com

P. F. Chang's is a hip, contemporary chain featuring regional Chinese food. Phantom loves the lettuce wraps served with garlicky chicken and a side of crisp iceberg "cups" for assembling at the table. Huge tables and family-style plates are ideal for group dining, while the Mongolian warrior sculptures create a fun atmosphere. Servers even mix dipping sauces tableside. Menu favorites include stir-fried salt-and-pepper shrimp, crispy honey chicken, and double pan-fried noodles with beef. If celebrating a birthday, order the six-layer Great Wall of Chocolate for the whole table to share.

THE GREATEST: Dessert Course

Finale $$
1 Columbus Ave., Boston, MA, (617) 338-3095
www.finaledesserts.com
Finale insists that dessert comes first. The elegant desserterie serves light meals and hot toddies, but it's the gorgeous cookies, cakes, and chocolates that are the main course for most diners. They're open late for the post-theater crowd, perfecting signature dishes like molten chocolate cake and crème brûlée smothered in six kinds of fresh fruit. Phantom favors the bittersweet Manjari mousse and the Boston cream pie served with mini whoopie pies. Locations include Harvard Square and Coolidge Corner in Brookline.

THE GREATEST: Wine Bar

Troquet $$$
140 Boylston St., Boston, MA, (617) 695-9463
www.troquetboston.com
Overlooking the Boston Common, Troquet has Boston's best by-the-glass wine selection. The unique menu gives unprecedented attention to the vintage pours over the food: 48 wines are listed down the center, with compatible dishes off to the side. Customers are encouraged to pick their drink first and then pair it with dinner. Wines can be sampled in two- and four-ounce pours, and there are 350 by the bottle. The kitchen prepares fabulous wine-friendly food like vanilla poached lobster and crispy duck confit with figs.

THE GREATEST: Happy Hour Menu

McCormick & Schmick's $$
34 Columbus Ave., Boston, MA, (617) 482-3999
www.mccormickandschmicks.com
McCormick & Schmick's is a seafood-steak house with outrageously cheap happy hour food. Theatergoers can swing by before the show 3:30 to 6:30 p.m. (weekdays) and every day from 10 p.m. to midnight for the social-hour menu at the bar, when snacks cost just two to four dollars. In addition to half-pound cheeseburgers

with fries, changing selections include steamed mussels in garlic chili broth, clam shooters, cheese quesadillas, chicken wings, bruschetta, and oysters on the half shell.

THE GREATEST: **Trendy Italian**

Teatro $$
177 Tremont St., Boston, MA, (617) 778-6841
www.teatroboston.com

Teatro is a stunning space where the ornate barrel ceiling casts a soft blue hue. The fine Northern Italian cuisine includes thin-crust pizza topped with hot peppers and sea salt. Rigatoni with ragu Bolognese is a meaty highlight, and the grilled rib eye sizzles with Gorgonzola butter. Most of the high decibel buzz comes from the bar, where the well-heeled sip one-of-a-kind cocktails like the Lemoncello-laced Carlini Tini. Teatro's Web site links to all the local playhouses, so customers can check show times and plan a reservation accordingly.

THE GREATEST: **Fine Dining**

Pigalle $$$
75 Charles St. South, Boston, MA, (617) 423-4944
www.pigalleboston.com

Pigalle gets pre-theater applause for fine dining dishes where familiar ingredients are whipped into something deliciously surprising. The classy menu is seasonal with French, Mediterranean, and Asian influence. The tuna tartare sparkles on an iced scallop shell, and other specialties include the rib eye steak frites au poivre and the butternut squash tortelloni with duck confit. Pigalle features a handsome black-and-tan setting with curved leather banquettes, vintage chandeliers, and beaded sconces. Settle into the six-seat bar for inexpensive eats from one of Boston's top kitchens.

North of Boston
GREAT ATE

THE GREATEST: Oyster Bar

Finz $
76 Wharf St., Salem, MA, (978) 744-8485
www.hipfinz.com

Finz takes full advantage of a waterfront location on Salem's Pickering Wharf. Whether sipping colorful martinis on the patio or slurping oysters by the fireplace, you'll be within eyeshot of Salem Harbor, which surrounds the restaurant on three sides. The spacious, modern dining room features a sofa lounge and a copper bar, and menu prices are incredibly reasonable for such high quality and creativity. Phantom's favorite dishes include Finz's famous Stoli-wasabi oysters, the spicy Buffalo calamari, and baked lobster stuffed with crabmeat, shrimp, and scallops.

THE GREATEST: North Shore Steak House

Gavens $$$
119 S. Main St., Middleton, MA, (978) 774-0500

Gavens is a stylish suburban steakhouse, offering prime cuts of meat and an extensive collection of wine. There's nothing "small town" about this fine dining restaurant. It's dark and intimate with plaid curtains and framed mirrors. The menu salutes Prime steaks, seafood, and fine chops like luscious lamb. Phantom likes to lead up to a New York strip steak with Alaskan king crab legs. No worries if you ingest some garlicky side dishes; there's Listerine in the bathroom.

THE GREATEST: Greek Cuisine

Ithaki $$
25 Hammatt St., Ipswich, MA, (978) 356-0099
www.ithakicuisine.com

Ithaki serves the finest Greek and Mediterranean food on the North Shore, often featuring garlic and fragrant herbs like oregano and rosemary. Fresh flavors are found in classic dishes like moussaka, or baked eggplant and lamb in creamy béchamel. The dolmadakia, or stuffed grape leaves, hide a tender filling of beef, rice, and herbs, while the grilled octopus appetizer sits on a bed of greens with tart lemon aioli. Lemony Greek-style roast lamb is a sight to behold, stacked with roasted potatoes.

THE GREATEST: **Affordable Seafood**

SeaWitch Restaurant & Oyster Bar $$
203 Newbury St. (Rte. 1 N.), Peabody, MA, (978) 535-6057

The SeaWitch is completely casual, comfortable, and affordable. Customers order straightforward seafood dishes at the counter, grab a number and a booth, and wait for the food to be delivered to the table. All selections are served grilled, broiled, or fried. No fancy sauces or sides are necessary when the fresh catch comes straight from the water. Notable dishes include the delicate fried clams, spectacular swordfish, baked stuffed clams, and broiled haddock.

THE GREATEST: **North Shore Italian**

Donatello $$
44 Broadway (Rte. 1), Saugus, MA, (781) 233-9975
www.donatello-restaurant.com

In an area where spaghetti and meatballs dominate Italian menus, Donatello stands out for authentic, inventive cuisine. It's inviting to both the casual crowd and sophisticated diners and features a dining room and bar that are bright and airy. Phantom's favorite antipasti are the fried calamari tossed with spicy pepper rings and the carpaccio with shaved Parmesan. The crispy pizzettes are topped with combinations like shrimp and sun-dried tomatoes or sausage, potatoes, and peppers. The spicy fusilli with lobster is awesome, and the double-thick chops (veal or pork) are massively satisfying.

THE GREATEST: **Upscale Mexican**

Cilantro $$
282 Derby St., Salem, MA, (978) 745-9436
www.cilantrocilantro.com

Cilantro is an elegant Mexican restaurant with an upscale twist. The whole red snapper is a rare treat of garlicky fish and skillet-crisped skin, while the spicy filet mignon is draped in chorizo and Chihuahua cheese. The handsome dining room displays a brick and wood interior that's perfect for a date. Café Cilantro is their casual sister establishment offering fast, affordable eats. A Taste of Cilantro around the corner focuses on takeout like burritos and tacos.

THE GREATEST: **Weekday Prix Fixe**

Catch $$$
34 Church St., Winchester, MA, (781) 729-1040,
www.catchrestaurant.com
Catch is . . . well, quite a catch! The cozy bistro turns out incredible seafood like
braised Maine lobster towering over a crispy risotto cake or seared scallops with
raisins, capers, and almonds. Incredible desserts include Bananas Foster Cheesecake and Meyer Lemon Mousse with raspberry shortbread. The weekday prix fixe
tasting is an excellent three-course deal available Tuesday through Thursday. The
dining room is elegant casual, and six coveted counter seats overlook the copper
pot kitchen.

THE GREATEST: **Soup**

Stone Soup Café $$
0 Central St. Ipswich, MA, (978) 356-4222
The homey Stone Soup Cafe is a laid-back eatery where breakfast and lunch are
walk-in and largely takeout. Fancier dinners on Thursday, Friday, and Saturday re-
quire reservations, often weeks in advance. White linens and flickering candles ro-
manticize the mood, and servers recite the menu since the bistro fare changes every
night. Dishes might include roasted scallops or the rack of lamb, and there's always
a selection of signature soups. Clam chowder is a perennial award winner, but
other standouts include tomato bisque, curried butternut squash, Cuban black bean,
Italian wedding, and pasta e fagioli.

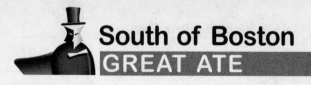

South of Boston
GREAT ATE

THE GREATEST: **Dessert for Breakfast**

Pogo's II $
657 Monponsett St. (Rte. 58), Halifax, MA, (781) 293-3939
Pogo's II is a breakfast bonanza where much of the menu is inspired by dessert.
Deep-dish French toast gets a lift from fluffy lemon meringue, and the blueberry
cheesecake pancakes are outdone only by the creamy, sweet tiramisu French toast.
The whopping six-pound Philly cheesesteak omelet is loaded with sliced sirloin,
onions, and peppers, and the meat lover's omelet is bursting at the seams with linguica, maple sausage, kielbasa, ham, bacon, and cheese. Pogo's II offers 16 fresh
baked breads like cinnamon raisin, Dutch chocolate, and San Francisco sourdough.

THE GREATEST: **Waterside Dining**

Back Eddy $$$
1 Bridge Rd., Westport, MA, (508) 636-6500
www.thebackeddy.com
Whether you arrive by boat or by car, the Back Eddy is the ideal summer restaurant.
It's a classy clam shack that takes full advantage of local farms and fishermen in
modern dishes like sausage-stuffed clams with Tabasco aioli. Giant seared scallops
are wrapped in applewood-smoked bacon, and the yellowfin tuna steak takes on an
Asian theme with wasabi, soy sauce, and kimchi. The light, airy atmosphere in-
cludes a patio bar, so you can have a Guinness just feet from the ocean.

THE GREATEST: **South Shore Bistro**

Coriander $$$
5 Post Office Sq., Sharon, MA, (781) 784-5450
www.corianderbistro.com
Coriander is an elegant, unfussy dining room where exciting, innovative cuisine
comes with personalized service. A husband-and-wife team puts on quite a dinner
show, where local ingredients prevail in gorgeous French dishes. The menu is always updating, with seasonal offerings like braised short ribs with tomato fondue,
and sliced steak with onion jam. Over-the-top desserts include house-churned ice
cream and the three-chocolate ganache cake with white chocolate sauce. To top it
all off, expect a personal visit from the chef.

THE GREATEST: **Wood Oven Italian**

Tosca   **$$$**
14 North St., Hingham, MA, (781) 740-0080
www.eatwellinc.com
Housed in a 1910 Granary Marketplace, Tosca is a dramatic setting of exposed brick, mahogany beams, and lofty ceilings. Using New England seafood, the open kitchen remains devotedly Italian with frequent use of a blazing wood oven. Smoky flavor is infused into pastas, roasts, and cracker-thin pizzas topped with porcini mushrooms and asparagus. The fontina and chicken lasagna is the richest Phantom has ever tasted, and the succulent slow-cooked Long Island duck "two ways" pairs a brown sugared breast with a cured and braised leg.

THE GREATEST: **Ice Cream**

Crescent Ridge Dairy   **$**
355 Bay Rd., Sharon, MA, (781) 784-8446
www.crescentridge.com
Crescent Ridge Dairy is a picture-perfect dairy bar where families can stroll with their cones along a white picket fence. Green pastures roll away in the background, while headlights and Little Leaguers flood the parking lot. The classic line up of scoops, sundaes, and frappes features 31 flavors of ice cream and five flavors of frozen yogurt. The sweetest treat is the wild blueberry sundae of ripe fruit swirled through the creamiest vanilla ice cream Phantom has ever licked. If you can't make it to the farm, Crescent Ridge offers home delivery from their very own milkman!

THE GREATEST: **Greek Salad**

Christo's   **$$**
782 Crescent St., Brockton, MA, (508) 588-4200
Christo's built its legendary reputation on a world-famous Greek salad. They start with crisp greens, cured olives, ripe tomatoes, and plenty of feta cheese. But what sets theirs apart is the homemade salad dressing that's so secret, even Phantom doesn't know all the ingredients. Other Hellenic favorites include juicy shish kebabs, baked lamb, crispy white pizza, and homemade baklava. Christo's is a massive complex with five dining rooms and a seasoned wait staff that won't flinch when you ask for extra feta.

THE GREATEST: Middle Eastern Menu

Byblos $$
678 Washington St., Norwood, MA, (781) 762-8998

Byblos may be the most delicious, authentic, and affordable Middle Eastern restaurant on the South Shore, and possibly in all of New England. Lebanese music plays in the background while customers feast on dishes laced with fresh herbs and olive oil. Traditional cuisine like hummus and baba ghanoush fly out of the kitchen along with sizzling grilled kebobs. The tabbouleh is a lemony grain salad with ripe tomatoes and parsley, and the crunchy fattoush salad combines cucumbers, scallions, radishes, and toasted pitas.

THE GREATEST: Rustic Escape

Red Lion Inn $$$
71 Main St., Cohasset, MA, (781) 383-1704
www.redlioninn1704.com

The Red Lion Inn rekindles romance in a country French setting of low wood-beamed ceilings, candelabras, and crackling fireplaces in each of four dimly lit dining rooms. A glass-encased kitchen is framed in copper pots, and the New England menu offers a great variety of native seafood. Favorites include the steamed Prince Edward Island mussels in luscious lemon cream, baked stuffed lobster, and potato-crusted cod in fresh thyme beurre blanc. The inn is a spectacular setting for weddings, and diners can extend their evening with a luxury guest room fitted with a Jacuzzi.

Metro West
GREAT ATE

THE GREATEST: Fine Comfort Food

Chiara $$$
569 High St., Westwood, MA, (781) 461-8118
www.chiarabistro.com

At Chiara, you can fine dine without the pressure to dress up. Past the fireplace lounge and alcove bar, the handsome wood setting looks like it's straight out of Pottery Barn. However, an exhibition kitchen under spotlights reminds diners that they're there to eat. The bistro menu is so fresh, it changes every six weeks with selections like homemade potato gnocchi in sweet garlic cream. The herb-crusted chicken with three-cheese cannelloni is Phantom's ideal comfort food, and one-of-a-kind desserts include the signature chèvre cheesecake with a gingersnap crust.

THE GREATEST: East Meets West

Blue Ginger $$$
583 Washington St., Wellesley, MA, (781) 283-5790
www.ming.com

Blue Ginger sets one heck of a high standard for quality, stylish dining outside of the city. Ming Tsai's inventive "East meets West" cuisine and his celebrity chef buzz make for an unforgettable meal that might kick off with tea-smoked salmon or their famous foie gras shumai dumplings in shallot broth. Superlative entrées like sake-miso marinated butterfish and the garlic–black pepper lobster are like nothing you've ever tasted. From the 40-foot blue pearl granite counter lining the open kitchen to the new communal bamboo table for 10, Blue Ginger stands apart.

THE GREATEST: Bodacious BBQ

Firefly's Bar-B-Q $$
235 Old Connecticut Path, Framingham, MA, (508) 820-3333
www.fireflysbbq.com

Firefly's is a fun BBQ house where low and slow cooking is an art. Hickory, cherry, and apple woods smoke the meats, which are packed with intensity from dry spice rubs. For added flavor, the condiment bar includes five sauces (North or South Carolina, Memphis, spicy Beelzebar, Texas), assorted pickles, and 40 hot sauces. The best appetizer platter combines ribs, wings, brisket, catfish fingers, and homemade chips. And the grilled cracklin' bread is awesome topped with onions and smoked mozzarella.

THE GREATEST: New American Menu

Fava $$
1027 Great Plain Ave., Needham, MA, (781) 455-8668
www.favarestaurant.com

How could a restaurant with flavors this bold be located in Needham's subdued town center? That's what Phantom kept asking himself as he tasted forkful after exciting forkful of their New American cuisine. The intimate neighborhood restaurant is located in a former train station, and diners can still embark on a spontaneous adventure with dishes like pan-seared scallops over sweet pea risotto. They also do a lovely lobster shepherd's pie and a porcini-crusted rib eye. The food, waitstaff, and atmosphere are completely unpretentious.

THE GREATEST: Suburban Steak House

Coach Grill $$$
55 Boston Post Rd., Wayland, MA, (508) 358-5900
www.coachgrill.com

The Coach Grill is a fine steak house with a dark wood interior of black leather banquettes and equestrian art. Stone fireplaces flank the lively rooms, and stately lamps suspend from the recessed ceiling. Steaks are aged for five weeks, and count on an expanded menu of chops, seafood, rotisserie selections, and a fine wine list. Phantom recommends the porterhouse steak with excellent marbling on the top loin side and butter knife tenderness on the filet mignon side. Servers in tan butcher jackets deliver a strong, smooth performance with rolling cart presentation of each course.

THE GREATEST: Upscale Indian

Masala Art $$$
990 Great Plain Ave., Needham, MA, (781) 449-4050

Masala Art is a hip Indian eatery where colored silk cushions light up the window seats and glowing lamps are carved into the wall. The lengthy blue-lit bar features a backdrop of mythical Indian characters that pop out in 3-D. Regional Indian cuisine draws from the chef's extensive spice library in all kinds of vegetarian, chicken, and lamb dishes. Masala Art also claims to have the nation's only spice bar, where customers can dig into a multicourse prix fixe while learning about Indian cuisine from the chef. He cooks right before your eyes with spices mixed to your exact specifications.

THE GREATEST: Roadside Diner

Harry's $$
149 Turnpike Rd., Westborough, MA, (508) 366-8302
www.westborough.com/harrys
Harry's is a roadside luncheonette with brown vinyl booths, baby stools at the
counter, and some of Phantom's favorite diner food. It's a solid value for breakfast,
lunch, and dinner, but stick to what they do best: fried clams and ice cream. The
Big Belly Plate looks like an ale-colored mountain of deep-fried clams coated in
just enough gritty batter to seal in the clam juices. For dessert, order a Big
Gulp–sized frappe or a brownie sundae piled high with hot chocolate sauce, home-
made whipped cream, and mini chocolate chips.

THE GREATEST: Asian and Italian

Maxwell's 148 $$$
148 E. Central St., Natick, MA, (508) 907-6262
www.maxwells148.com
Maxwell's 148 is properly sophisticated for a savvy, suburban clientele. Cream and
bronze tones create a relaxing atmosphere, enhanced by crystal chandeliers, thick
velvet curtains, and hydro rock gardens. The fascinating copper-plated menu alter-
nates among Italian, French, and Asian dishes loaded with flavor and texture. Every
meal starts with a basket of large Chinese noodles and fresh breads, and it only gets
better with standouts like eggplant curry in a clay pot, the Big MAX Rib Eye with
Tuscan fries, and lobster pad Thai.

Central and Western

GREAT ATE

THE GREATEST: Fine Dining

Wheatleigh   **$$$**
Hawthorne Rd., Lenox, MA, (413) 637-0610
www.wheatleigh.com
Prepare to be pampered as you roll into the luxury isolation of Wheatleigh, a boutique hotel and restaurant in the Berkshires. Dining is an exquisite treat in the glass-encased portico appointed with soaring Greek columns. Guests settle on velvet chairs and savor artful plates like citrus-cured halibut and venison tartare with horseradish and baby beets. The menu is delightfully constrained to ingredients at the peak of harvest, and after the cheese trolley rolls around, superb desserts like a sorbet tasting or the Manjari chocolate soufflé cap off the evening.

THE GREATEST: Pizza by the Slice

Antonio's Pizza   **$**
31 North Pleasant St., Amherst, MA, (413) 253-0808
Antonio's Pizza is a late night favorite for UMass students in search of a cheesy Sicilian slice. Until 2 a.m. on weekends, college kids mob the counter in this skinny pizza shop, ogling the 20-plus pies on display. Antonio's has mastered 300 kinds of pizza, and about 50 of these exotic varieties are available each day. Outrageous creations include black bean and avocado, lasagna, chicken blue cheese, and tortellini. There's a second Antonio's in Providence, Rhode Island.

THE GREATEST: German Restaurant

Hofbrauhaus   **$$**
1105 Main St., West Springfield, MA, (413) 737-4905
www.hofbrauhaus.org
For Wiener schnitzel, sauerkraut, and strudel, the Hofbrauhaus is the closest to Munich you can get in Massachusetts. German pictures and beer steins decorate two dining rooms, and the waitstaff wearing German dresses delivers a variety of Bavarian specialties. The deep-fried sauerkraut with corned beef and cheese is simply outstanding. One bite of the sauerbraten with potato dumpling and red cabbage is like taking a trip back to the Old Country, and outstanding German beers like Schneider Weisse and Paulaner Thomasbrau top off the experience.

THE GREATEST: **Fairground Food**

The Big E $
1305 Memorial Ave., West Springfield, MA, (413) 737-2443
www.thebige.com

The Big E is an autumn tradition and the ninth largest fair in North America. One million people pass through the gates every September for glorious gastronomic gluttony. The highlight is the deep-fried dream world, where everything imaginable gets a hot, golden garb. Count on corn dogs, Oreos, and vegetables to take the Frialator plunge. Phantom's favorites are the deep-fried candy bars, which emerge with a crunchy seal around gooey, melted chocolate. Check out the Avenue of States for local specialties from Rhode Island, New Hampshire, Maine, Vermont, and Connecticut.

THE GREATEST: **Cajun and Creole**

Chef Wayne's Big Mamou $$
63 Liberty St., Springfield, MA, (413) 732-1011

For the taste and feel of authentic New Orleans, Phantom heads to Chef Wayne's Big Mamou. Cajun and Creole fare include the specialty of the house: puff pastry baked around crawfish, shrimp, and veggies in lobster cream sauce. Other enormous entrées include shrimp and sausage jambalaya and pork loin stuffed with sausage cornbread filling. Make room for Bourbon Street Cheese Bread and Jerked Thunder Thighs. Surrounded by Louisiana murals and stuffed alligators, Chef Wayne's is all about eating and fun. The menu is BYOB, and some customers bring their own blenders for homemade margaritas!

THE GREATEST: **Tunnel Bar**

Tunnel Bar $$
125A Pleasant St., Northampton, MA, (413) 586-5366

Like the name implies, this ultra-cool bar is located inside a 100-foot-long, 12-foot-wide railway tunnel that dates back to 1896. The trains stopped running years ago, and now the only sidecars you'll find here are mixed to order. The wine list reads like a book, and the mixologists serve 200 martinis on weekend nights. For nibbling, there's shrimp cocktail, a fruit and cheese tray, and warm toasted nuts. Due to the romantic atmosphere, the dim lighting, and no-cell phone access (due to a stone foundation that's six feet deep), Tunnel Bar has earned its reputation as the "tunnel of love."

THE GREATEST: Herbal Dining

The Herb Lyceum at Gilson's $$$
368 Main St., Groton, MA, (978) 448-6499
www.gilsonslyceum.com

From a gorgeous country retreat, the hosts at the Herb Lyceum at Gilson's open their nineteenth-century carriage house for "herbal dining." The four-acre property grows over 300 varieties of herbs, which show up in creative dishes every Friday and Saturday night. The BYOB six-course tasting menu is reservations only with limited seating. Guests arrive early to stroll the gardens before gathering at a communal table for what feels like a fun dinner party. Incredibly fresh dishes might include crispy salmon with chive emulsion or tuna tartare with cilantro pesto.

THE GREATEST: Seafood in Central Massachusetts

The Sole Proprietor $$
118 Highland St., Worcester, MA, (508) 798-3474
www.thesole.com

The Sole Proprietor is a fine seafood restaurant with a hip bar scene. The long, varied menu reads like a delicious novel, with tempting chapters devoted to sushi, oysters, and lobster. Inventive specials include the shrimp macaroni and cheese, maple-glazed scallops, and roasted mako wrapped in prosciutto. The vibrant bar is always buzzing thanks to flirty cocktails like strawberry mojitos and the sangria bowl. Every summer, an inflatable crustacean named Buster the Crab commandeers the restaurant's roof. He's 75 feet long and 12 feet tall, and during his stay the Sole Proprietor offers crab specials.

Cape Cod
GREAT ATE

THE GREATEST: **Tasting Menu**

Chillingsworth $$$
2449 Main St./Rte. 6A, Brewster, MA, (508) 896-3640
www.chillingsworth.com

Set in a 300-year-old mansion, Chillingsworth is designed for wining and dining. Every guest orders from the seven-course tasting menu, interspersed with palate cleansers like chilled plum soup and grapefruit sorbet. Following appetizer oysters in puff pastry, entrées might include the saffron swordfish steak or seared lamb with roasted tomatoes. Fancy desserts such as the chocolate hazelnut crisp with praline ice cream top off the feast, along with coffee, tea, or cappuccino. Antiques and period wallpaper underscore the Colonial character of each intimate room, and six acres of gardens surround the property.

THE GREATEST: **Bar Scene**

RooBar $$
586 Main St., Hyannis, MA, (508) 778-6515
www.theroobar.com

To escape the Cape without leaving the peninsula, RooBar is the place. Nothing about it screams flip-flops and lobster print pants, and the trendy atmosphere draws a young, trendy crowd. Additional locations in Chatham, Falmouth, and Plymouth are just as sleek and sexy, yet each pioneers its own modern menu. Adventurous eaters can try cinnamon steak, tuna parfait with cilantro lime sorbet, banana-encrusted halibut, and soy-candied spiced ribs. RooBar makes crazy-delicious pizza topped with duck confit, spiced lamb, or a balsamic glaze.

THE GREATEST: **Clambake**

Lobster Pot $$
321 Commercial St., Provincetown, MA, (508) 487-0842
www.ptownlobsterpot.com

The Lobster Pot juts out over the water, offering two floors of clambake dining. The upper level "Top of the Pot" is the perfect place for cocktails as the sun goes down in P-town. The seafood menu ranges from traditional clam chowder to innovative pesto oysters. Portuguese specialties like linguica sausage-crusted cod expand the options, though Phantom's favorite is the pan-roasted lobster in brandy butter. Amazing desserts include Key lime pie and a mint chocolate chip ice cream sandwich slathered in chocolate sauce.

THE GREATEST: Ice Cream Parlor

Four Seas Ice Cream $
360 South Main St., Centerville, MA, (508) 775-1394
www.fourseasicecream.com

Four Seas is a vintage ice cream parlor with authentic soda shoppe character, from swivel stools to old-fashioned dipping cabinets. They have the longest running ice cream tradition on the Cape, featuring 34 flavors like fresh strawberry, chocolate chip cookie dough, and maple walnut. They even claim to have invented chocolate chip ice cream! Instead of cheap sprinkles, load up on homemade sauces like butterscotch, walnuts in maple syrup, and classic hot fudge. Root beer floats and extra-thick frappes are classic as can be.

THE GREATEST: Fine, Fine Dining

Twenty-Eight Atlantic $$$
Wequassett Inn, Rte. 28 Pleasant Bay, Chatham, MA, (508) 430-3000
www.28atlantic.com

Twenty-Eight Atlantic is exorbitantly pricey, but it's worth every cent for the cutting-edge menu and panoramic views of Pleasant Bay. The high-end atmosphere feels as exclusive and cosmopolitan as a Park Avenue eating club, set with oversized tables and a nautical décor. The luxury cuisine hones in on fresh local seafood and often drips in delicacies like caviar butter, oxtail ragout, truffles, and foie gras buttons. Intricate platings of caramelized scallops nest in a golden potato "basket" over pillows of peekytoe crab, and the braised lamb shank pairs with pumpkin polenta.

THE GREATEST: "Moving" Dinner

Cape Cod Central Railroad $$
252 Main St., Hyannis, MA, (508) 771-3800
www.capetrain.com

The Cape Cod Central Railroad is a truly unique "all aboard" experience that combines a scenic choo-choo ride with a gourmet lunch, brunch, or five-course dinner. The vintage train chugs along a 46-mile, three-hour journey, while the converted kitchen prepares everything onboard in an old baggage car. To partake, get your caboose to Hyannis Station and embark on an elegant evening of creamy seafood chowder and entrées like lobster-stuffed haddock. While barreling over the Cape Cod Canal, move onto silky raspberry chocolate cheesecake. The three-course lunch is less formal, and there's a Family Supper Train that caters to kids.

THE GREATEST: **Romantic Dining**

Red Pheasant Inn $$$
905 Main St., Dennis, MA, (508) 385-2133
www.redpheasantinn.com

The Red Pheasant Inn is nestled in a barn that's nearly as old as the nation. The cozy setting is borne out in wide plank floors, exposed beams, and two blazing fireplaces. Their private garden contributes edible flowers and fragrant herbs, which show up in the New England fare. The kitchen is best known for the rack of lamb cooked in port wine, rosemary, and garlic, but they also prepare a game special nightly, along with duckling, local seafood, and aged beef.

THE GREATEST: **Oyster Bar**

Naked Oyster Bistro & Raw Bar $$
20 Independence Dr., Hyannis, MA, (508) 778-6500
www.nakedoyster.com

Naked Oyster captures the essence of Cape Cod dining with fresh fish preparations and a raw bar featuring a dozen varieties of oysters. The shucked shells come "naked" and raw or "dressed" and cooked. Barbecued Bleu Oysters are rich and delicious, embedded with Great Hill Bleu cheese, caramelized onion, and BBQ sauce. The Bienville take on mushrooms, garlic, shrimp, and bacon, and the Baked Oishi Oysters perk up with pickled ginger and wasabi. The Mediterranean are smooth, combining Gaeta olives, feta, and spinach. The handsome setting sports an ocean theme, and curvy oyster lamps add to the classy look.

Providence
GREAT ATE

THE GREATEST: Tuscan Cooking

Siena $$$
238 Atwells Ave., Providence, RI, (401) 521-3311
www.sienaprovidence.com

Siena is a gorgeous little town in Tuscany, and now it's also a gorgeous little restaurant in Providence. Free valet parking and solid service are big boons to this Federal Hill favorite, but authentic Italian cuisine is what keeps customers pouring through the door. Diners enjoy Tuscan soul food like pasta e fagioli, the famous garlic cannellini bean soup. Stuffed portabello caps or a wood-grilled pizza make an excellent appetizer before some meaty pasta Bolognese or a seared skirt steak in Chianti wine sauce. The lively bar sports cheetah-print seats, while the back is more relaxed and romantic.

THE GREATEST: Rustic Fine Dining

New Rivers $$$
7 Steeple St., Providence, RI, (401) 751-0350
www.newriversrestaurant.com

At New Rivers, modern American cuisine meets old-world charm. Laid out like an intimate farmhouse, the adjoining rooms display pear portraits and twinkling white lights. Entrées come in two sizes, all with locally farmed fruits and vegetables. Waiters in jeans and button-downs deliver wild mushroom tarts with goat cheese and truffle oil. Other standouts include molasses-grilled ribs and sugar pumpkin tortelloni with homemade chicken sausage. The fresh-baked cookie plate is a highlight, and the ever-changing "chocolate dessert" is always rich and delicious.

THE GREATEST: Grilled Pizza

Al Forno $$$
577 South Main St., Providence, RI, (401) 273-9760
www.alforno.com

Al Forno is the famous inventor of grilled pizza, which claims more of a wood-smoked flavor than the oven-baked standard. The paper-thin crust wears a garlicky tomato sauce on pies like the Provençal, cooked over an open flame with black olive tapenade and goat cheese. The kitchen also turns out hot dishes like rigatoni with five-pepper sauce and the spicy clam roast. White tablecloth dining takes place on two elegant levels with an ivory downstairs and a second floor decorated in slate stone tiles.

THE GREATEST: Midnight Munchies on Wheels

Haven Brothers Diner $

Corner of Fulton and Dorrance streets, Providence, RI, (401) 861-7777

Haven Brothers in Providence is a mobile stainless steel diner on wheels. It rolls into City Hall every evening around 5 p.m. and plugs into an electric outlet that powers the grill until 4 a.m. Politicians and professionals stop by on their way home, followed by partygoers looking for a late-night snack. Phantom loves the All-the-Way Dogs (mustard, onions, relish, celery salt,) bacon cheeseburgers, and chili cheese fries. The messy Murder Burger is a double-decker piled with cheese, chili, bacon, mushrooms, onions, lettuce, tomatoes, and mayonnaise.

THE GREATEST: Half-Price Wine Mondays

Pane e Vino $$

365 Atwells Ave., Providence, RI, (401) 223-2230

www.panevino.net

At cozy, romantic Pane e Vino, an honest Neapolitan menu gets a lift from an incredible Italian wine selection. Monday nights are especially good for upgrading or experimenting, because the entire wine list is half-price. Classic dishes are the kitchen's strength, like roasted peppers heaped over fresh basil and mozzarella. The rack of lamb sits in a rich cherry demi-glace, and sausage teams with pancetta bacon in a rigatoni pasta dish finished with creamy pink sauce. For dessert, indulge in sorbet and Italian cookies, or homemade tiramisu.

THE GREATEST: Sandwich Menu

Geoff's Superlative Sandwiches $

163 Benefit St., Providence, RI, (401) 751-2248

Geoff's Superlative Sandwiches has a funky college atmosphere with a checkered floor, raised stools along the walls, and exposed brick. There's even a pickle barrel smack in the center of the room; customers serve themselves unlimited dill spears. The chalkboard menu lists 100 quirky sandwiches with playful names like Jaws (tuna salad, melted cheese), the "Slim" Jim O'Neil (lettuce, tomato, onion, sprouts, horseradish), and the Godfather (hot pepperoni, Genoa salami, Provolone, pepperoncini oil). Or enlighten Geoff's with your own invention on seeded rye, wheat, pumpernickel, or a bulky roll.

THE GREATEST: **Hot Steak House**

XO Steakhouse $$$
125 North Main St., Providence, RI
www.xocafe.com

XO Steakhouse is hot and trendy with racy sculptures and graffiti walls to spice up the atmosphere. They even pipe random sounds into the bathroom. With a motto of "Life is short, order dessert first," the restaurant breaks all the norms. The red meat menu kicks off with fluorescent cocktails, followed by Black Angus steaks. Each cut, including the espresso-rubbed hanger steak, comes with sauces like the tamarind XO. And their french fries are outrageously delicious, tossed with truffle oil and Parmesan cheese.

THE GREATEST: **Trendy Dining**

Mediterraneo $$$
134 Atwells Ave., Providence, RI, (401) 331-7760
www.mediterraneocaffe.com

Mediterraneo combines fine Italian dining and sexy, urban atmosphere. Giant French doors and striking cherrywood bars add to the trendy vibe. Steaks, seafood, and pasta modernize with their flashy presentation, but it's the antipasti bar that makes the biggest impression. The spread changes daily, including items like prosciutto, sharp provolone, sautéed eggplant, red and yellow peppers, bean salad, potato croquettes, arancini rice balls, olives, and mushrooms. There's a special "cravings" menu of panini and grilled pizza in the sidewalk café, and on Friday and Saturday nights, the second level transforms into a Latin dance club.

Phantom's
88 TASTY TIPS

1. Don't bother asking the waiter what's good on the menu; ask what *isn't* good instead. You'll get a laugh, and a more honest answer.

2. When you buy coffee past noon at Dunkin' Donuts, ask for one Munchkin. They often throw it in for free. In fact, Phantom once got 14 for no charge.

3. Prix fixe menus are a great way to sample an expensive restaurant for less. Phantom's favorites are at Sel de la Terre, Upstairs on the Square, and Craigie Street Bistrot.

4. Keep in your planner or handheld a list of eight restaurants you've been meaning to try. It'll come in handy when you need to make plans on the fly.

5. The Cape Cod Potato Chip factory in Hyannis is a fun way to spend a rainy day. The free, self-guided tour concludes with a free bag of Phantom's favorite chips (www.capecodchips.com).

6. If you want to try a really expensive restaurant on the cheap, eat at the bar.

7. The best way to "top" a hot dog is to "bottom" it. Place your ketchup, mustard, onions, and relish on the bun, under the link. This technique is a lot neater and provides a truer frank flavor.

8. If you hate to share or often experience "dinner envy" of your dining partner's dish, play it safe and order exactly the same thing.

9. When you go to the Phantom Gourmet Food Festival, enter on the Ipswich Side of Lansdowne Street. You'll get in much quicker than on Brookline Avenue (www.phantomgourmetfoodfestival.com).

10. Parking in Chinatown can be a pain, but King Fung Garden on Kneeland Street has a handful of free spaces. Plus, their Peking ravioli and scallion pancakes are the best in the neighborhood.

11. Au Bon Pain has an evening bake sale offering 50 percent off pastries. Hours vary according to location.

12. Spicy foods cool the body down naturally, which is why most spicy cuisines come from hot countries like Mexico, India, and China.

13. Each cut of steak has its merits, but generally it's a tradeoff of tenderness for flavor. Looking for buttery texture? Filet mignon is for you. Something with more heft and succulence? Order a strip steak. Best of both worlds? The porterhouse is your cut.

14. The chains are now too chicken to serve burgers less than medium, so hit the small independent restaurants if you like yours rare.

15. *All* clam chowder in New England is "award winning," so don't pay any attention to such claims. Phantom likes the creamy version at Legal Sea Foods, and the thicker chowdah at Union Oyster House.

16. Your Chinese New Year's order should be made a minimum of three days ahead and kept to simple dishes. This is no time to experiment on steak kew. —*phantomlover, FEEDback Forum Member*

17. Even Phantom has trouble making reservations at some hot restaurants. Sometimes the best way to get in is to show up and ask for a table. Restaurants typically set aside a few seats for VIPs and hotel concierges.

18. If you like tail meat, ask for a female lobster. If you like the claws, order a male. And if you just don't care, order a lobster roll.

19. Zon's in Jamaica Plain rewards the hard-working restaurant world with "Industry Wednesday." Prove you're in the business with a pay stub or a uniform and pay half-price for your food.

20. Until you double-check that you got everything on your takeout or delivery order, do not pay.

21. Stop at the Sausage Guy on Lansdowne Street on your way into a Red Sox game. It's a tastier link at a superior value than you'll find inside Fenway Park.

22. To practice proper sushi etiquette, dip the fish, not the rice, in the soy sauce. Rice acts like a sponge, drowning out the delicate seafood. But flip it over, and you'll get just the right salty accent to draw out the fresh flavor.

23. Avoid dinner theaters; neither the dinner nor the theater tend to be good.

24. When ordering pizza at Pizzeria Regina in the North End, act like a local. *Do not* pat the grease off the pie like the tourists; instead, drizzle the house-infused olive oil across the top.

25. WaterFire is a "moving sculpture" that takes over downtown Providence in the summer. From May to October, the floating bonfires illuminate a half-mile stretch of three rivers. Spectators make dinner reservations at outdoor restaurants along the way (www.waterfire.com).

26. Always order to the strength of the menu. Sushi from an Irish pub is *never* a good idea.

27. Ask the server for the specials. He or she may forget to mention them, and you'd find the neighboring table enjoying that Phantastic dish you didn't even know you could order.

28. It pays to tip generously anywhere you're a regular. Aside from great service, often you'll find a few extras on the plate.

29. Morton's is a fine dining steak destination, but their Bar 12*21 offers one of the best bargains in Boston. Monday through Friday, from 5 to 6:30 p.m., they serve a "Bar Bites" menu for as little as $1.50 per plate. Phantom's picks are the filet mignon sandwiches and fresh oysters.

30. True heat seekers head to East Coast Grill & Raw Bar during their Hotter Than Hell Nights. The fiery festival is held twice a year with devil-horned waitresses serving red-hot dishes like pasta with habanero sausage and Tabasco bananas.

31. Beware of restaurants that say their ice cream is homemade. Ask if they churn it on the premises. If it's made in someone else's kitchen, it's not homemade.

32. When you discover a great new restaurant, grab two take-out menus: one for the house and one for your car. That way, you'll always be prepared to pick up dinner on the way home from work. —*Eric Sherman, PG Senior Producer*

33. Kowloon hosts their legendary Lobsterfest at the beginning of the calendar year and again in early summer. Beyond buttery twin lobsters, customers can crack into rarely seen lobsters dishes like scallion and ginger, Szechuan, Chinese-style, spicy tomato, black bean sauce, and Thai-style.

34. Relive the Italian feast from the movie *Big Night* at Grotto in Beacon Hill. This special event happens a couple times a year. Dressed in '50s evening wear, guests indulge in everything from timpano to whole roasted pig.

35. Resist the tiramisu temptation after a big North End dinner, and stroll the neighborhood's many dessert shops. Modern Pastry makes the best cannoli, Gelateria scoops out awesome Italian ice cream, and Caffe Vittoria froths the top cappuccino.

36. Worcester isn't called "Diner City" for nothin'. The very first "night lunch wagon" was launched in 1872, and you can still find plenty of classics like Paul Mac's Diner on Shrewsbury Street.

37. The quickest way to offend a real Jewish deli is to ask for your bagel toasted. If it's truly fresh, the extra heat will destroy the chewy texture. If you know it's day-old or not made in-house, then request it well done.

38. Beard Papa's in Faneuil Hall is best known for cream puffs, but they also bake an incredible chocolate fondant cake. It's so good that Boston's best restaurants could charge five times as much.

39. Across the street from the Back Eddy in Westport is the Way Back Eddy. Stop by in your bathing suit and bare feet to fuel up on gourmet grub like pulled pork sandwiches, homemade chips, and extra-thick milkshakes.

40. If you see "butterfly" on the steak house menu, don't start squirming. The cooking term refers to a cut down the center of a thick steak or shrimp so it splits nearly in two, cooking quicker and more evenly.

41. When ordering a burger for takeout, ask for one temperature degree less than you really want it. Since it will continue to cook on the ride home, it'll be just the way you like when it's time to eat.

42. If you like condiments as much as Phantom does, keep a spare stash of squeeze packets in your glove compartment. It's like striking gold when the drive-thru forgets to toss some in the bag.

43. When reading the fortune cookie, add the words "at the buffet" at the end. For example, "You will be fortunate in everything you put your hands to . . . at the buffet!" After two Mai Tais, try adding "in bed."

44. Day-old bread is great for making French toast, but when it comes to sandwiches, fresh is the only way to roll. Ask your neighborhood bakery for its oven schedule.

45. Never let a waiter top off your coffee. It throws off the ratio of brew to cream to sugar. To avoid computing fractions over breakfast, finish your entire cup and wait patiently for a complete refill.

46. If you want to beat the brunch buffet, skip the pastries, muffins, and bagels at the front of the line. The "high-rent district" omelets and carving stations sit at the end of the spread.

47. Over 125 of Boston's best restaurants take part in Restaurant Week at the end of the summer and winter. For just over $20 at lunch and $30 at dinner, you get a complete three-course prix fixe meal (www.bostonusa.com/RestaurantWeek).

48. Pressing down on a patty with a spatula results in a dry, flavorless burger. Seek out the grill cooks who leave their plump burgers to sizzle and stay juicy.

49. Die-hard chocoholics may think they've melted and gone to heaven on The Old Town Trolley Boston Chocolate Tour. The conductor offers chocolate trivia while making several tasting stops in the city's best kitchens (www.trolley tours.com/chocolatetour).

50. White breast meat is the most popular cut of chicken in America. But around the world, the chicken thigh is the king of clucks. It has a little extra fat, but thigh meat is much more flavorful.

51. Do a dry run before a big date! Check the parking situation, confirm the reservation, request a secluded table, scan the online wine list, and check the reservation list to make sure none of your exes will be sitting at the booth next to you.

52. Ask your server to give your unfinished bottle of wine to the kitchen. They'll appreciate the tip and possibly return the favor with free food.

53. The first thing you should do when entering a diner is look up. If the staff takes the time to keep the ceiling clean, chances are they're keeping the kitchen spic and span, too. —*Randy Garbin, author of* Diners of New England

54. Craving a lickety-split intermission snack in the Theater District? Dominic's (255 Tremont Street) is a total dive with no special menu, but it's perfect for grabbing a quick, cheap slice before the show or between acts.

55. When ordering steak, tell the chef to cook it however he thinks it will taste best. The chef probably does know better than you, and even if he doesn't, he'll be so appreciative that you're likely to get the best cut. —*Ernie Boch Jr.*

56. There's usually a local eatery in every mall food court. Give it a try. You never know which Frank's Pizza is destined for national expansion.

57. At drive-thru windows, always over-order by at least 20 percent. Chances are they'll forget something, so if you want four burgers and nine chicken nuggets, ask for five burgers and twelve nuggets. And don't forget to ask for sauce and ketchup!

58. To eat like a true Italian, order a pasta course (primi) between the antipasti and the entrée (secondi). Restaurants are usually happy to halve their pasta portions, so this three-course tradition won't weigh you down.

59. The skinny on all the squares in Cambridge is that each has its own dining style. Try Harvard for fine dining, Inman for fun date places, Central for ethnic eats, and Kendall for pub grub.

60. Dairy products like milk and yogurt help cut the spiciness if you overdose on chili peppers. Those without the spice tolerance of Phantom's palette should steer clear of the pepper's interior veins and seeds, where the heat is concentrated.

61. There's often a surcharge for eating outdoors, but it's worth the splurge if you dine as the sun sets.

62. Vodka and soda is a Phantastic low-carb cocktail. To add flavor, squeeze the lime and "muddle" it on the bottom of the glass with the cocktail straw. —*Dave Andelman, PG CEO*

63. The best way to reheat leftover pizza is on a pizza stone in a 500-degree oven. But when Phantom is in a hurry, he skips the microwave, which results in a soggy crust, and pops it in the toaster oven or on a dry stove-top skillet.

64. Try ordering your next sandwich *Phantom-style.* That means double meat, double cheese, and potato chips stacked inside for added extra crunch.

65. The Porter Exchange (1815 Massachusetts Avenue) in Porter Square, Cambridge, hides a strip of Asian restaurants and shops offering everything from sushi to Korean food to ramen noodles and stir-fries.

66. Phantom recommends trying seafood specials on Friday and Saturday night, when the chef probably found Phantastic specimens at the fish market. But skip them on Sunday and Monday, when the restaurant might be trying to move weekend leftovers.

67. Ask soup servers to ladle from the bottom of the pot, where the ingredients are closer to the flame and all the good stuff tends to sit.

68. During the fall and winter, it's better to enjoy heavier drinks like Johnnie Walker scotch to warm up from the cold weather. When the temperature heats up around spring and summer, switch to something refreshing like Tanqueray and tonic.
—*Arnold Baer, Phan*

69. Half-bottles are creating the biggest buzz in the wine world since the Pinot Noir explosion from the movie *Sideways*. These manageable pours make it easy and more affordable to have white with the appetizers and red with the entrées.

70. If you don't want to shell out $20 for valet parking in the Back Bay, try parking at the Prudential Center Garage. Spend $5 in the mall (which Phantom usually does at the food court) and ask the sales associate to stamp your parking ticket. You'll save much more than that on discounted validated parking.

71. One of Phantom's favorite snack foods is the crispy, crunchy noodles served in Chinese restaurants. An industrial-sized bag from Chinatown costs $5 and, with a little duck sauce for dipping, it's the ultimate Asian "chip and dip."

72. For an exciting twist at McDonald's, dip the burgers in the sweet and sour Mc-Nugget sauce. —*phantomlover, FEEDback Forum Member*

73. In some states, it is legal to bring leftover wine home. Ask the manager if you're unsure.

74. Olde Dutch Cottage Candy on Tremont Street is the most mysterious store in the South End. This candy store/antique shop/florist is rarely open, but it's the only place in town where you can find chocolate truffles, Liberace portraits, and silk roses under one roof.

75. Don't be shy about asking for a special table. The right seating can turn a celebration into something unforgettable, and make or break a first date.

76. Scan the bill before you pay. Phantom has found enough incorrect charges to buy a small country. Same goes for takeout and delivery.

77. If you're not good with chopsticks, ask for the kid version. Welded together at the top, they're much easier to use.

78. When ordering at a steak house, calculate the number of side dishes by dividing the total human pounds in your party by 200 and rounding up. For example,

4 men × 300 pounds = 1,200 pounds (six sides), and 3 women × 100 pounds = 300 pounds (two sides).

79. While it is illegal for restaurants in Massachusetts to have "happy hours" with deals on drinks, many have "appy hours" with inexpensive appetizers at the bar. —*Kim Driscoll, PG Senior Editor*

80. The Alamo in Milford serves amazing Mexican food. Plus, you might just run into Dewey from *Malcolm in the Middle*; his family owns the restaurant.

81. Pigalle in the Theater District is a fine French restaurant, but the bar menu offers inexpensive eats from the same skilled kitchen. Instead of dropping $200 in the dining room, spend $20 noshing on Malaysian chicken wings, mac and cheese, fish and chips, and pork buns.

82. Every day of the week has a different vibe in a restaurant. Monday and Tuesday are relaxed and better for family dining, the executive chef usually runs the show on Wednesday and Thursday, and Friday and Saturday are lively but tough to get special attention.

83. Order your toasted bagel before your coffee so it can cook while they pour the cup of joe.

84. Heinz is the world's best ketchup. Hit the "57" on the side of the bottle, and the red stuff pours out like magic.

85. Many restaurants are closed on Monday, but they often host wine dinners or cooking classes. The cost is usually relatively cheap and you get dinner, wine, and a unique evening. —*Sean Finley, PG VP of Visual Media & Production*

86. There's almost always a wait at RedBones in Davis Square, but the best seats in this BBQ house are at the counter in the back. They're often available, and the kitchen hands out free snacks like garlic sausage.

87. Although the food is just okay, Phantom enjoys the chef show at places like Benihana and Bisuteki. Spend a few bucks to upgrade from white rice to fried rice, and clap for the chef so he'll give you any extra shrimp.

88. Treat every customer like a critic. You never know which one could be the Phantom Gourmet.

Index of Restaurants by Location

Flat Patties, 23
Formaggio Kitchen, 150
Frank's Steakhouse, 34
Garden at the Cellar, 149–150
Harvest, 67
Helmand, The, 51
Henrietta's Table, 20
Hi-Rise Bread Company, 38
Iggy's Bread of the World, 6–7
L.A. Burdick Chocolate, 33
Midwest Grill, 83
Miracle of Science Bar + Grill, 149
Oleana, 40, 149
Om Restaurant & Lounge, 151
Picante Mexican Grill, 101
Pinocchio's, 109–110
Rendezvous, The, 151
Salts, 115–116
Sugar & Spice, 150
Upstairs on the Square, 62
Z Square, 104

Charlestown/Bunker Hill

Cold Stone Creamery, 84–85
Figs, 27
Olives, 122
Tangierino, 114
Warren Tavern, 124

Chestnut Hill

Bernard's, 30
Chocolate Dipper, 72
Metropolitan Club, 127–128
Oishii Sushi Bar, 129–130

Chinatown

Buddha's Delight, 154
Eldo Cake House, 153
Ginza, 131, 153
Jumbo Seafood, 152
King Fung Garden, 152
News, 92
Peach Farm, 154
Penang, 153
Shabu-Zen, 152
South Street Diner, 91
Tomasso Trattoria & Enoteca, 88

Dorchester/Roxbury/Jamaica Plain

Ashmont Grill, 66
Boston Speed Dog, 79

café D, 132
dbar, 92
El Oriental de Cuba, 119
M&M Ribs, 11
Pit Stop Barbeque, 75
Restaurante Cesaria, 52–53
Simco's on the Bridge, 79
Real Deal, The, 75
Vintage, 33–34
Zon's, 97

Downtown

Ándale!, 100
Café Fleuri, 7
Locke-Ober, 12
Peking Tom's, 31
Pizza Oggi, 133
Pressed Sandwiches, 58
Silvertone, 35
Sultan's Kitchen, 53
Cosi, 54–55
Four's, The, 137
Via, 29

East Boston

Belle Isle Seafood, 120
Kelley Square Pub, 110
Santarpio's Pizza, 108–109
Taqueria Cancun, 52

Faneuil Hall

Beard Papa's, 74
Boston Chipyard, The, 36
Dale & Thomas Popcorn,
    123–124
Durgin-Park, 12
Houston's, 25–26
Plaza III, 50
Seasons, 62
Union Oyster House, 14

Fenway

Audubon Circle, 137
Eastern Standard, 122
El Pelon, 99–100
Game On! 63–64
Petit Robert Bistro, 40–41
Sol Azteca, 99
UBURGER, 21–22

Alphabetical Index

New England Soup Factory, 33
New Rivers, 182
News, 92
Ninety Nine Restaurant & Pub, 135–136
No Name Restaurant, 121
No. 9 Park, 146–147
Nordic Lodge, 81
Not Your Average Joe's, 124

O

Oak Room, 128
Oarweed, 95
Odyssey Cruises, 63
Ogunquit Lobster Pound, 94
Oishii Boston, 130
Oishii Sushi, 129–130
Oleana, 40, 149
Olives, 122
Om Restaurant & Lounge, 151
O'Natural's, 59
On the Border, 125
Orinoco, 132
Osushi, 131
Outback Steakhouse, 24
Out of the Blue, 121

P

Pane e Vino, 183
Panera Bread, 25
Panificio, 147
Papa Gino's, 57
Papa John's, 55
Paragon, 140
Paramount, The, 15, 147–148
Parish Café, 135, 143
Parker's Maple Barn, 4
Party Favors, 7
Pastiche Fine Desserts, 7
Peach Farm, 154
Peking Tom's, 31
Penang, 153
Persy's Place, 15
Petit Robert Bistro, 40–41
Petsi Pies, 39–40
P. F. Chang's, 25, 164–165
Pho Republique, 90
Picante Mexican Grill, 101
PICCO, 86, 163
Pigalle, 166
Pinocchio's, 109–110
Pit Stop Barbeque, 75
Pizza Barn, 138–139

Pizza Oggi, 133
Pizzeria Regina, 108
Plaza III, 50
Pogo's II, 170
Polcari's Coffee Shop, 158
Popeye's Chicken & Biscuits, 56
POPS, 104
Potbellies Kitchen, 102
Pressed Sandwiches, 58
Prezza, 156
Publick House, The, 96

Q

Quan's Kitchen, 32
Quizno's, 55

R

Real Deal, The, 75
RedBones, 9
Red Lion Inn, 172
Red Pheasant Inn, 181
Red Robin, 68
Red Rock Bistro, 18–19
Red Wing, 70
Rein's Deli, 138
Rendezvous, The, 151
Restaurante Cesaria, 52–53
R. F. O'Sullivan's Pub, 21
Richardson's Ice Cream, 84
Richie's Slush, 86
Risorante Fiore, 49–50
Rockmore Floating Restaurant, 105
Ron's Gourmet Ice Cream and 20th Century
    Bowling, 84
RooBar, 28, 179
Roof Top Pool, 105
Rosebud Diner, 43–44
Rosie's Bakery, 38
Roy Moore Lobster Co., 93–94
Ruth's Chris Steak House, 126

S

Sabur, 53
Sal's Pizza & Italian Restaurant,
    81–82
Salts, 115–116
Salumeria Italiana, 159
Sam LaGrassa's, 117
Santarpio's Pizza, 108–109
Sasso, 103
Seasons, 62
SeaWitch Restaurant & Oyster Bar, 168